PRO BITCOIN OFFLINE VAULT
SERVERLESS WALLET – BA.NET

**How To Safeguard Your Bitcoins
With Your Own Offline Vault**

Mar 2016

Bitcoin Offline Vault and Serverless Wallet - BA.net (c) BA.net
iphone@ba.net android@ba.net ba.net/bitcoin

Chapter 7 to 11 derived from of Bitcoin.org, Wikipedia.org with GNU
Documentation License.

The optional software ba.net/bitcoin is licensed MIT open source and
(c) ba.net

1 WHY BUY BITCOINS?

Many people have heard of Bitcoin, but far fewer understand why someone would want to buy bitcoins. "What is it used for?", "Why not use a credit card?" and other questions are common. So, here are the main reasons people just like you buy bitcoins.

1.1 ONLINE SHOPPING

Buying products and services online is often cheaper, faster, and results in higher overall customer satisfaction than other options. Unfortunately, credit cards and paypal can put limitations on what you can buy, from where. Growing costs paid to combat fraud and identity theft are passed onto you when you use them but are largely eliminated with Bitcoin.

1.2 PRIVACY

Identity theft is among the greatest costs to society. To combat identity theft, people subscribe to identity protection services and online shops require lots of personal info. Bitcoin payments can be trusted by the shop with no additional personal information. That means, unless you're getting something shipped to you, you may not even need to provide your name or address when shopping. Bitcoin is not anonymous but if additional steps are taken, nobody but you and the merchant are likely to know what you buy online.

1. 3 PERSONAL FREEDOM

Nobody can limit who you send your bitcoins to. Visa, Mastercard, and PayPal block payments to perfectly legal businesses, some political organizations, and to anyone that may bring them legal or PR problems. Bitcoin payment is a protocol that doesn't care who you're paying or why.

1.4 FINANCIAL INDEPENDENCE

When handled securely, Bitcoin can be even better than gold for savings. The exchange rate of early Bitcoin versus other currencies is volatile. If Bitcoin is successful at growing in usage, most of that volatility will increase its price and make you money. The fact remains that your bitcoins cannot be bailed-in or seized without your cooperation. You can even store bitcoin using a password that only you know. This places more power back in your hands to become financially independent.

1.5 LIMITED QUANTITY

There will only ever be twenty-one million bitcoins as sure as we all agree that 2 + 2 = 4. Contrast this with central banks around the world that create money with the click of a mouse. Bitcoin reduces monetary policy to a straightforward schedule.

1.6 Current and Future Valuation of Bitcoin

We argue that Bitcoin is currently not primarily valued as a medium of exchange or transactional currency, but as a gold-like store of value and speculative investment (an excellent one, if you agree with Peter Thiel that it has a 20% chance of going mainstream - a 20% chance of 100x or 1000x growth), and why this is not a bad thing.

It is important to distinguish between the reason for Bitcoin's present valuation and the reasons it will likely be valued in the future. For example, the fact that Bitcoin will probably save online retailers a lot of of money in the future makes Bitcoin valuable not as a currency now, but as an investment now and a currency in the future. It is easy to misinterpret the fact that its *future* as a currency is largely what is driving its current valuation to mean that it is right now, today, valued largely because it enables transactions. People buying bitcoins now because they believe they will be sought out for transactional purposes *in the future* is not the same as people buying bitcoins now because they are sought out for transactional purposes *now*.

Investors who understand Bitcoin's potential do it an important service. They inform the public, through price information, of that which most of the public is unable or unwilling to figure out on their own: that Bitcoin has tremendous potential to change the world and warrants serious attention, both currently for certain people as a hide-able, unconfiscate-able, transportable, no-third-party-risk store of wealth and in the future for everyone as a transactional currency.

Just because it turned out to be better for the "store of value" function first is no reason to worry overly about the transactional function taking time to blossom - that's what investors are for. The ones that invest based on a sound assessment of Bitcoin's future potential serve as a proxy for actual present commercial adoption by boosting the price in the present to a degree commensurate with how likely commercial adoption will be to take hold in the future.

Prematurely using commercial adoption as a measuring stick for Bitcoin's success doesn't really make much sense. Bitcoin is a many-splendored thing, and is valued by investors for both its current and future uses.

2 BITCOIN WALLET BA.NET

2.1 A Bitcoin Wallet

A Bitcoin wallet is as simple as a single pair of a Bitcoin address with its private key. A wallet has been generated for you in your web browser and is displayed above.

2.2 BA.NET BITCOIN WEB WALLET

The easiest way to send a receive bitcoins without installing any software. No need to register username, email or any info.

Create a Bitcoin address, private key, experiment, test away. All code runs on your own web browser and does not depend on any central server. You are in control.

2. 3 TO SAFEGUARD THIS WEB WALLET

You must print or record the Bitcoin address and private key. You can use the My Address Webapp.

Make a backup copy of the private key and store it in a safe, separate location. This site does not have knowledge of your private key.

If you leave/refresh the site or press the "Generate New Address" button then a new private key will be generated and the previously displayed private key will be lost.

2. 4 ADD FUNDS

Add funds to this wallet by telling people to send bitcoins to your Bitcoin address. Make sure you made a backup copy of the private key.

2. 5 CHECK YOUR BALANCE

You can check your balance using the BA.net Bitcoin Web Wallet or by going to blockexplorer.com and enter your Bitcoin address.

2. 6 SPEND YOUR BITCOINS

Spend your Bitcoins using the Send Bitcoin Option.

Remaining change will be sent back to the sending bitcoin address (source address). Simple.

The amount of bitcoins you can spend will be checked before sending. Use the view history button for details. If the address has transactions pending with 0 confirmations, you will have to wait to send funds. 1 confirmation is enough to send bitcoins.

You can set the miner transaction fee to any value you choose. or 0.

2. 7 ADVANCED MULTISIG WALLET

You can create a private key with 3 components. Send the 3 components to 3 friends. And 2 friends are required to create an usable private key to spend the bitcoins. Also called split wallet.

Click on Multisig for split wallets and more advanced features. Cold Storage, Paper Wallet, Brain Wallet, BIP38 Encrypt, Bulk Wallet, Vanity Wallet and more.

If you don't have the private key, you don't own Bitcoin. Be your own bank Design Objective.

2.8 OFFLINE (OR AIR-GAPPED) BITCOIN TRANSACTION

An offline Bitcoin transaction is created with a computer that is not connected to the Internet (or any network). Assuming the installation process was secure the computer can not be reached by hackers.

3 DESIGN OBJECTIVES

If you don't have the private key, you don't own Bitcoin. If you store the key on someone else's server, even if encrypted, your key is not safe. Be you own bank.

3.1 PRIVATE KEY LOSS IS CATASTROPHIC

The primary problem is that losing a key means that all bitcoins stored with that key are lost forever. The way to deal with this is: Create keys frequently and destroy them as soon as they are no longer needed

3.2 MITIGATE RISK BY HAVING MORE KEYS FOR SHORTER DURATIONS

A more secure mitigation against key loss is to generate new addresses/keys frequently, use them for specific operations, and then destroy them.

For example, when traveling, create a new **Travel Key** and use that until you are back home. That way if anyone compromises your travel laptop or phone they only breach the compartment for the duration of your travel.

The impact of the compromise is contained by the limitation on the utility of the key.

For storing bitcoins create a cold paper wallet. You can create your address/key on a computer with no Internet connection. Air-gap computer running the ba.net serverless wallet.

3.3 Why use Offline Bitcoin ?

Computer security is hard. Physical security is much easier to accomplish.

Using Offline Bitcoin allows you to store your wealth securely in an offline vault. Your own vault that you control physically.

You can transfer needed amounts to online wallets on your phone or computer. Bitcoin is just like cash, you should only carry around spending money.

3.4 DO NOT TRUST SERVERS WITH YOUR KEYS

If you don't have the private key, you don't own Bitcoin. If you store the key on someone else's server, even if encrypted, your key is not safe. Be you own bank.

Backup your keys in different locations. You can keep them encrypted with a password.

3.5 SERVERLESS WALLET SIMPLICITY ADVANTAGE

Spend Your Bitcoins using the Send Bitcoin Option. Remaining change will be sent back to the sending bitcoin address (source address).

This allows you to make the backup of your key at the creation time only. As opposed to, backing up your wallet all the time on a downloaded wallet. Downloaded wallets create a new change address for each transaction. This is the reason for confusion and the need of constant backups.

The BA.net serverless Wallet needs only one backup when you create it!

3.6 DOWNLOADED WALLETS LIMITATIONS

You can download a bitcoin client and import your private key. Note that on downloaded bitcoin clients, usually remaining change goes to a new address. That is why Satoshi recommended never to delete a wallet!

3.7 Bitcoin Address and Private Key Reuse

When you reuse your Bitcoin Address you reveal your balance and transaction history of that address to your counterparty. Losing financial privacy.

Another un-desirable problem is that for each use there is a hash signature on the blockchain generated with the private key. There is a theoretical attack exploting information from this signatures. This attack has not been seen yet, but it could be possible.

So both for privacy and security, bitcoin addresses should not be reused. Especially for large amounts of coins.

4 BITCOIN OFFLINE TRANSACTIONS

4.1 WHY OFFLINE BITCOIN ?

Computer security is hard. Physical security is much easier to accomplish.

Using Offline Bitcoin allows you to store your wealth securely in an offline vault. Your own vault that you control physically.

You can transfer needed amounts to online wallets on your phone or computer. Bitcoin is just like cash, you should only carry around spending money.

4.1 WHAT IS AN OFFLINE BITCOIN TRANSACTION ?

An offline Bitcoin transaction is created with a computer that is not connected to the internet (or any network). Assuming the installation process was secure the computer can not be reached by hackers.

To create a Bitcoin payment the offline machine can create a Bitcoin transaction which can then be carried by an USB key. This information can then be copied to a machine that is online, and the transaction can be broadcast.

Your private key never touches the Internet. Maximum Security.

4.2 HOW DO I CREATE AN OFFLINE TRANSACTION ?

Use the PRO Bitcoin Wallet and Vault BA.net App. Search for "banet" at the Apple AppStore for OSX.

Also available on iPhone, iPad, or Flashboot Software Appliance

 Featured by Apple on top 10 Finance Apps

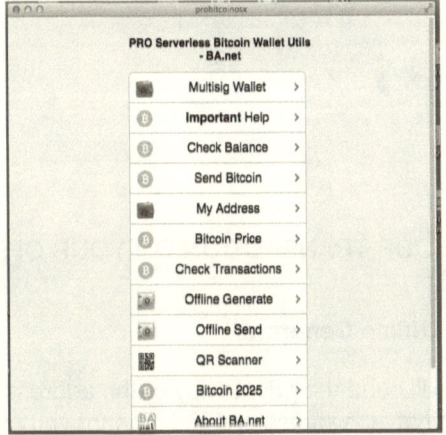

4.3 Retrieve Unspent Outputs

Retrieve the unspent outputs for your bitcoin address. Use the button Send Bitcoin (the regular online send bitcoin) paste your source address and **click view history**

You need to cut and paste this info into a text file and transfer it to the USB key.

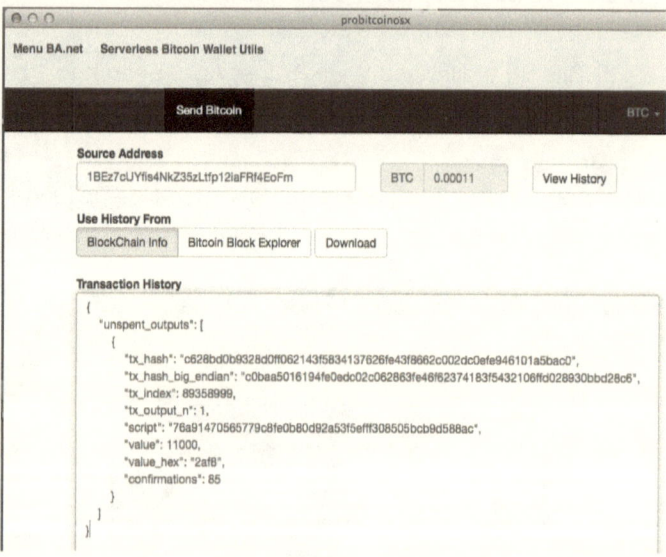

4.4 CREATE YOUR TRANSACTION ON YOUR OFFLINE MACHINE

Use the button **Offline Generate**.

To do this you will need the private key of the address you want to send from, destination address and the amount you want to send.

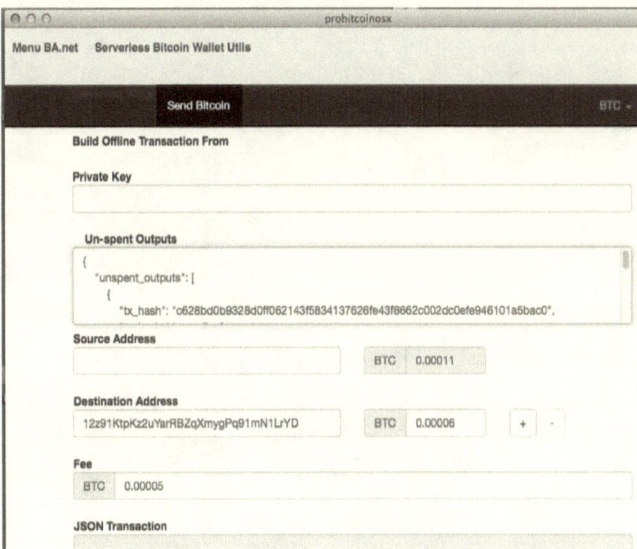

Cut and Paste the values into the form and generate a transaction. Cut and the paste the generated transaction RAW HEX from the form field into a text file and place it on your USB key.

4.5 SUBMIT THE TRANSACTION TO THE BITCOIN NETWORK

Use the button **Offline Send**.

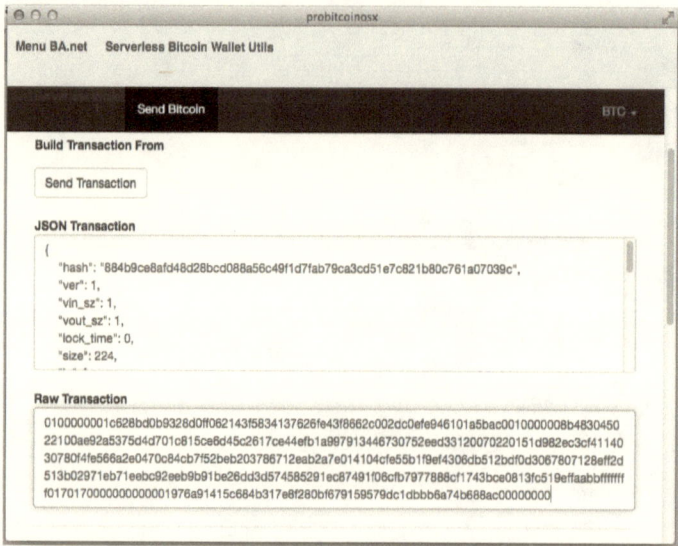

At no point in this process is the private key data exposed through the transaction data. Your private key never touches the internet, for maximum security.

The biggest threat to an offline wallet is an USB-key virus that executes when plugged in. However, such viruses would have to be highly targeted, and can be mostly mitigated by disabling USB-auto-run on the offline computer.

Alternatively, you can transfer this information using the new QR Code Generator Option. No networking of any kind needed.

4.6 TAKE TIME TO GET FAMILIAR WITH THE PROCESS

It is normal to be uneasy using new software to store your savings, especially with advanced features. Make a few offline transactions with new addresses/keys and small amounts of bitcoins.

After a couple of offline transactions you will be doing them in less than a minute. You will be able to say that you are your own bank!

4.7 Bitcoin Address and Private Key Reuse

When you reuse your Bitcoin Address you reveal your balance and transaction history of that address to your counterparty. Losing financial privacy.

Another un-desirable problem is that for each use there is a hash signature on the blockchain generated with the private key. There is a theoretical attack exploting information from this signatures. This attack has not been seen yet, but it could be possible.

So both for privacy and security, bitcoin addresses should not be reused. Especially for large amounts of coins.

For offline cold wallet storage the simplicity of having only one address/key to backup is important. As well as not having any more change addresses to add complexity. Once the coins come out of cold storage it is best practice not to reuse addresses.

---

5 UNIQUE BITCOIN ADDRESSES

5.1 BITCOIN ADDRESSES

Bitcoins are 'stored' in something called **bitcoin addresses** - they look something like
this: 1j2m5TakK99HvJUTfg2b2b8EGWQenmdTh. There are two parts to a bitcoin address – the public key (commonly just called the address) and the private key – the important part that lets you spend the bitcoins on its corresponding public key. Bitcoin is an example of public key encryption, as you can give out the public key freely but you must keep the private key to yourself.

To send bitcoins to an address, a message is broadcast from the owner of the sending address to the network that X amount of coins from that address now belong to the new address. This operation is authorized by the sender's private key, and if he doesn't have the private key he can't spend the coins, plain and simple.

Bitcoin addresses are created by first picking a random number (for the all important key) and creating an ECDSA (Elliptic Curve Digital Signature Algorithm) public / private key pair with them. This operation alone generates the private key – but Bitcoin addresses are not simply public keys, but rather modified versions of them. The generated public key is then put through several SHA-256 and RIPEMD-160 operations, until eventually being converted into a format called Base-58. Base 58 is an encoding that removes the possibility of similar looking characters, such as lowercase L and uppcase I, as well as 0 and O. Finally an identifying number is added to the beginning of the address – for most bitcoin addresses, this is generally 1, indicating it is a public bitcoin network address.

It is infeasible though technically possible that two different people could generate the same bitcoin address. In such a case, both would be able to spend the coins on that particular address. The odds of this happening are however so small that it is not going to happen in the next couple million years. If you're skeptical, read Why is 2^256 Secure for a stern talking to regarding the security and wonders of exponential growth.

5.2 Why is 2^256 Secure

There's always a lot of talk about the security of modern cryptographic hash functions, mainly SHA-256. This is a hash function used to verify a lot of important stuff – modern website logins are hashed with it, and Bitcoin relies on it almost entirely. There's always a lot of confusion regarding the safety of the function – as we know in the past things are found to be insecure after being declared 'absolutely secure' a few years prior to them being broken. Why is this particular iteration of hash functions so perfect?

The main problem with this idea is how poorly the human mind can understand the exponential function. Our brains can wrap around the concepts of addition and multiplication fine – but when we get to exponents our minds have trouble wrapping our heads around how quickly numbers get unimaginably big.

So what exactly is 2^256? Well, if we're being technical...

115792089237316195423570985008687907853269984665
640564039457584007913129639936

So – for all those doubting the security of 2^256 collision chances, there's the number: There is a 1 in over 115 quattuorvigintillion (that's a 78 digit number) chance of finding a collision. Note: In practice it's actually SLIGHTLY higher than that, due to something called the birthday problem, however the difference is so abysmal that it's hardly worth accounting for.

It's a freaking huge number. This number is bigger than the number of atoms in the perceivable universe. And not by just a little bit either. Exponentially bigger. This number is so big that the human mind can't comprehend how big it is. It's just really big. Huge. I can not overstate this enough. This is a very big number. Your financial and cryptographic transactions are secure because of how big this is. Only a fool would attempt to brute force this many possible combinations.

So why is this particular number now big enough to be secure for the significant future? Well, it's partly because we've simply increased the exponent to the point where the numbers get ridiculous, whereas before (with hash functions such as MD5, we were being a little cautious with a 'just enough' approach to exponential security. A brute force attack on with this many combinations is infeasible to a crazy degree. Does that mean it's impossible for someone to find the same hash as someone else? No. It's not mathematically impossible. It never will be – that's how numbers work. If a number exists, anyone can find it. However, at this point it's no longer worth peoples time trying – because it would take hundreds of millions of years to MAYBE get a result. That doesn't even guarantee the result they're looking for, just A result.

Is it technically, for the sake of mathematics, possible? Yes. Will we ever witness it in a meaningful way? Absolutely not going to happen. Probably.

5.3 Private Key Generation with Code

We use an open-source client-side keypair/wallet generators. The code is open and audited by the community. Heavily tested and trusted versions are included in the apps releases for local execution.

The code includes several sources of entropy from the users's computer, and from mouse movement input, and keyboard input.

5.4 Private Key Generation with Dice

The apps also provide the option of using Dice. An important part of creating a Bitcoin wallet is ensuring the random numbers used to create the wallet are truly random.

Physical randomness is better than computer generated pseudo-randomness. The easiest way to generate physical randomness is with dice. To create a Bitcoin private key you only need one six sided die which you roll 99 times. Stopping each time to record the value of the die. When recording the values follow these rules: 1=1, 2=2, 3=3, 4=4, 5=5, 6=0. By doing this you are recording the big random number, your private key, in B6 or base 6 format.

You can then enter the 99 character base 6 private key into the text field above and click View Details. You will then see the Bitcoin address associated with your private key. You should also make note of your private key in WIF format since it is more widely used.

5.5 An alternative Dice method

This private key generator requires two dice or any other randomizing method. Roll the two six sided dice 64 times. Right down the numbers like this: If the number is 0-9 right now the number. If the number is 10-12 right now a-c. Do this with each roll of the dice and you will get a valid hex private key, such as:

A9 87 3C 79 B6 D8 70 A0 1B 61 57 78 63 33 89 B4 45 32 13 30 3A A6 1C 20 CC 67 2C 23 36 B3 32 62

This is a valid bitcoin private key. Note that this does not use all the hex characters, and as such can not generate all possible private keys, but its easy to do with just two dice.

You could also buy a 16 sided dice or something and use 0-F which would be more proper. If you do it this way, the max address you can use is FFFF FFFF FFFF FFFF FFFF FFFF FFFF FFFE BAAE DCE6 AF48 A03B BFD2 5E8C D036 4141

6 BITCOIN COLD STORAGE

Cold storage – the storage of valuables, specifically bitcoins, in such a way that they are significantly harder to steal than normal, though at the admitted cost of delay in access times. There are a number of popular methods for performing such bitcoin storage, but to use most of them you still have to wade knee-deep into cryptography jargon and it seems like you need an advanced degree just to keep your coins safe. On this chapter you will find a simple introduction.

One of the bigger benefits Bitcoin has is its cash-like nature. People are used to cash, they understand cash much better than most digital payment systems, so let's make an analogy with cash. You take a million dollars cash to a bank and deposit it.

Would you be surprised at all if you returned to the bank a few months later and were told you'd have to wait a few days to withdraw your million dollars? Probably not. It's well-understood that your branch probably doesn't have enough cash on hand to cash out your million and still do business – they don't feel comfortable holding that kind of money in the same place they hold the smaller amount of cash they transact their daily business with – they have most of their money somewhere much more secure. Even the convenience store on the corner keeps a small amount of cash in the register and the majority of their money in a safe. Cold storage is the Bitcoin version of a safe.

The one tiny bit of terminology you need to understand to fully comprehend the basic concept of cold storage is what techies mean when they refer to systems, databases and other things as "hot" or "cold." A "hot" system is one that's live, running, connected. A "cold" system is powered-down, stopped, offline. To this end what we really mean when we say "cold storage" is that we're storing Bitcoins somewhere that's not connected to the Bitcoin network or, in most cases, even connected to the Internet or even on a computer at all.

There are a multitude of ways to do this, and we'll explore a few in detail, but it all boils down to the very basic principle that if your data isn't on a computer that's connected to internet then someone has to physically gain access to it to compromise it, and it's way easier to secure things physically than digitally.

So how do you ensure the safety of your coins? Most of the options people list fall (often incorrectly) into one of three categories:

6.1 PAPER WALLETS

Paper wallets are one of the most popular methods for storing bitcoins offline. A program of some kind generates the public and private halves of a Bitcoin address (or several). There are usually handy little barcodes that you can scan with your phone, so you don't have to type those monstrously long things in by hand when the time comes to use your coins. You print off what you've generated and send coins to that address.

You have just printed your very own paper money and it can be stored securely in exactly the same ways that cash can.
Update: It is worth noting that there are problems surrounding proper paper wallet use which, since the original publication of this article has led me to no longer categorize them as cold storage.

They are safer than most alternatives and so they remain in this article, but technically, they're not actually cold storage. Also, there's been an improvement called "BIP38" that means you can now make paper wallets with encrypted private keys. Should you choose any storage system involving paper wallets, you should absolutely choose to encrypt your private key.

6.2 BRAIN WALLETS

Brain wallets are a little more complicated. Where the addresses in paper wallets are generated at random, the addresses in brain wallets follow rules. You memorize something long and random, like a random sequence of words: "steady harbor business last barn test instant begun know silver driver naturally closer sum automobile some" would make a decent passphrase, for example. Again some piece of software comes into play and turns your passphrase into one or more Bitcoin addresses in a completely reproducible way.

There is something of a standard method for turning passphrases into addresses, but that would bring us knee-deep in jargon again. Via the standard method, our above passphrase would yield a Bitcoin address of "1Jkibvu28YqSiSqdyB9jgcAAJCRWqg2QQL" so we could send some coins to that address and as long as we can remember the passphrase. It's also incredibly important to have a long and secure passphrase for this method – longer than most can remember, which makes this method somewhat less popular. If someone can guess your password, they can steal your money.

This address, for example, was generated from the example passphrase from this comic. Someone used a pop culture reference to create their Bitcoin address and if there were actually funds there, we could all steal them now.

While proper brain wallets are now fading out of vogue, a similar technique is often used to back up newer deterministic wallets. A "seed" passphrase is used to generate many addresses so you only have to back one thing up to recover all of them, no matter how many you use. Again, though, this is technically offline key storage, not cold storage.

6.3 12 Words Seed

12 Words is a deterministic bitcoin address generator. Store bitcoin by writing down your 12 words and salt on a piece of paper. Address generation takes place in app, offline. No information is ever sent to the Internet.

It is preferable to write down the 12 words and salt rather than using a printer. Store your paper in a secure safe. For larger amounts make several paper copies on separate locations.

---

12 Words

Passphrase:

murder warm strong manage kitchen thrown peer eventually gain bound friendship stood

[random]

Salt:

more words

[generate]

Public Address (SHARE):

1KapVgc8cQvLqPu82KJ5szdyi1CReU956z

Disclaimer: Use at your own risk. Brainwallets can be dangerous if you don't use a strong passphrase or take security precautions.

Use a long, unique passphrase that is never used in any song, literature, or media. If you use a weak passphrase, you are at risk of having your bitcoin stolen. We recommend a minimum of 12 random words. Click the "random" button to have a secure 12-word passphrase generated for you. If you forget your passphrase, your bitcoin will be lost forever.

Your salts are used as additional inputs to the cryptographic function that generates your brainwallet. This information never gets sent to the Internet, and is only used to strengthen your passphrase. There is no recovery process, so don't forget what you enter.

12 Words uses the scrypt key derivation function to generate bitcoin addresses. Your salt inputs are concatenated and used as the salt for the scrypt function.

The process is as follows (pseudocode):

· key = scrypt(passphrase, salt, N=2^{18}, r=8, p=1, dkLen=32)
· keypair = generate_bitcoin_keypair(sha256(key))
Scrypt is a memory-intensive function that is deliberately slow to frustrate brute-force attacks. Performance may vary depending on your hardware, and in some cases may not work at all. If you run into problems, try a different web browser or use a newer computer. We can't sacrifice security for legacy support.

No Warranty

By using 12 Words, you are agreeing to the following terms and conditions.
The service is provided on an "as is" basis, without any warranties.
We are not responsible for any losses in bitcoin that you may incur for any reason.

6.4 COLD STORAGE / HARDWARE WALLETS

While the above are often called "cold storage" they're technically just offline key storage, which means they're only safe when used properly – and since they're basically never used properly, this is problematic. Since this article was first written, however, a new option has become available: True cold storage via hardware wallets. You can now simply buy a device that stores its own keys and does its own message signing all without every touching a potentially-compromised computer system. This is now the preferred method and should be used whenever it is an option since it doesn't require you to know or follow any kind of "best practices" for securing funds. Just use the device and you're good.

It's important to note that, under most circumstances, you generate these addresses, use them for storage once and then never use them again. In order to use the funds in a paper wallet, you have to use the account on an online (hot) computer, which lowers the security of whatever account you just used. Under most circumstances, such addresses should be considered to be single-use addresses only. Which way you should go is up to you, but I'll give you a few tools you can use either way.

First, bitaddress.org is an excellent and accessible tool. Despite looking like a normal web page with multiple tabs, the whole thing is written in such a way that once it's loaded it never needs internet access again. You can go to the page, completely disconnect your computer from the net and it will still work. You can even save a copy of the page to your hard disk and it'll still work locally – As a matter of fact, that's the way the most paranoid among us suggest you do this. Bitaddress.org is also fairly unique in that they offer a huge amount of functionality: they can generate paper wallets one address at a time or in bulk, they do brain wallets too and they even have a special "bulk wallet" function for people who want to accept payments on their web site without actually storing their coins on some scarily-insecure web server.

Users of the popular blockchain.info wallet service can also create a paper wallet through blockchain.info's "offline" functionality and as an added bonus, you can keep monitoring the funds in those accounts through the same site (and apps) you monitor your regular balances with. They even have a method for performing transactions with paper wallet addresses that doesn't "burn" the address – at least not as badly as any other method of spending from such wallets (they prompt you to enter they key and then use it once, never actually storing it).

6.5 OFFLINE BITCOIN TRANSACTION

An offline Bitcoin transaction is created with a computer that is not connected to the internet (or any network). Assuming the installation process was secure the computer can not be reached by hackers.

To create a Bitcoin payment the offline machine can create a Bitcoin transaction. This can be be carried by an USB key or other means to a machine that is online and the transaction can be broadcast.

Your private key never touches the Internet. Maximum Security.

6.6 HOW DO I CREATE AN OFFLINE TRANSACTION ?

Use the PRO Serverless Bitcoin Wallet BA.net App. Search for "banet" at the Apple AppStore for iOS or the MacStore for OSX

7 BITCOIN CHANGE ADDRESSES COMPLEXITY

Few topics in Bitcoin cause more confusion, anxiety, and loss of money than change addresses. They seem counterintuitive and unnecessary. They're a major contributor to wallet software complexity. When used improperly, they can de-anonymize not just the payer but other parties as well.

Given the many problems with change addresses, why do they exist in the first place? This article explains what change addresses are, why they're essential to Bitcoin, and how to protect your money and privacy.

TEST TIME

If change addresses seem confusing, you may be working under some false assumptions about how Bitcoin works. Try this simple test to see for yourself.

Alice buys Bob's computer for 1.05 BTC. Her wallet contains 2.23 BTC stored in a single address. Assuming no fee is involved, how much of Alice's money will be involved in the transaction?

- · A: 1.05 BTC
- · B: 2.23 BTC
- · C: Not enough information

If you answered A, then you may view Bitcoin as a kind of bank account in which a transaction debits an arbitrary amount of money from one account and credits it to another. This is a very common view that is unfortunately incorrect.

If you answered B, you probably know about change addresses, but don't understand why they exist. What you know isn't enough to prevent you from losing money in certain situations.

The correct answer is C: not enough information. After reading this article, you'll understand why this is the case and what information would be needed to find the exact amount of Alice's payment.

BITCOIN IS A CASH SYSTEM

Humans have been using cash for thousands of years, and cash is still important in most parts of the world. Every cash system assigns a face value to a token that can be used as payment. Paper bank notes and metal coins are examples of tokens we've all used since childhood.

Bitcoin is a cash system that replaces physical tokens with digital tokens called COINS (or more technically, unspent transaction outputs - UTXOs). When you receive a payment, you accept one or more of these digital coins. When you make a payment, you reassign ownership of one or more of your coins. A single address can hold multiple coins at the same time. Likewise, a transaction may gather coins from the same address, or multiple addresses.

Many cash transactions generate change. For example, if you pay for $64.89 worth of groceries with four $20 bills, the checker owes you $15.11 in change. To make a cash payment, we try to find enough bank notes to meet or exceed the payment amount. Any amount in excess of the required payment is returned as change.

The same holds true for Bitcoin transactions. Change is received by directing it to a designated change address. Change not recovered by a change address is claimed by miners as a transaction fee.

Bitcoin needs change addresses because Bitcoin is a cash system.

WALLETS REINFORCE MISCONCEPTIONS

Software wallets attempt to hide Bitcoin's deep connection to cash by presenting an interface similar to the one used by online banking services. Payment amounts appear to be deducted from your wallet balance and added to the wallet balance of your payee.

As we've already seen, this is not how Bitcoin transactions work. Instead, your wallet digitally signs and broadcasts a transaction to the network. The transaction reassigns ownership of one or more of your coins to your payee, returning any change to an address controlled by the wallet.

Although wallets handle change for you automatically, they can vary greatly in exactly how this is done. Failure to understand the differences can lead to confusion and loss of money.

WALLETS AND CHANGE ADDRESSES

Three main strategies for handling change have been adopted by wallet developers. Each one has different implications for privacy and security.

- **Single Address Wallets** use one address for receiving both payments and change. Addresses can be added by importing a private key or manually adding a new receiving address. Examples of Single Address Wallets include BA.net, Blockchain.info and MultiBit.
- **Random Address Pool Wallets** use a pool of randomly-generated addresses to receive payments and change. If a transaction generates change, it is sent to the next available unused address, causing a new address to be added to the pool. The best-known example of an Address Pool Wallet is Bitcoin Core.

- **Deterministic Address Pool Wallets** use a pool of deterministically-generated addresses to receive payments and change. Given a particular unique SEED, these wallets always generate the same sequence of addresses. Examples include Electrum and Armory.

Wallets can adopt new change-handling behavior depending on user settings and other state. For example, importing a paper wallet into MultiBit results in a two-key system in which change may alternately be sent to the original address and the paper wallet address, a situation with critical implications for security. Likewise, Electrum permits users to send all change to the same address, effectively creating a Single Address Wallet.

WHY NOT USE THE SAME ADDRESS?

It may seem odd that wallets would generate a new address to accept change. Why not return change to the same address? Why the apparently useless complexity of address pools?

The main reason is PRIVACY. By necessity, every Bitcoin transaction becomes part of a permanently viewable global ledger called the BLOCK CHAIN. Maintaining privacy in this system depends on a strict separation between addresses and personal identities, a model referred to as PSEUDONYMITY.

Imagine that a transaction moves a coin from Address A to Address B. If change is returned to the sending address, the block chain makes it trivial to deduce that the person controlling Address A paid the person controlling Address B. If two payments are made, both payees can easily be identified. And so on.

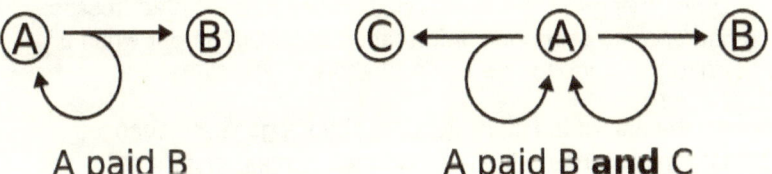

A paid B   A paid B **and** C

*The intended payee address can be trivially
determined when change is returned to the sending
address (left). Multiple transactions make it possible
to determine multiple payees unambiguously (right).*

An observer able to link a real-world identity to Addresses A, B, or C
may be able to deduce the identities of the other parties as well.

Now imagine that a transaction moves a coin from address A to
Address B, but directs change to Address C. Without additional
information, the only thing an outside observer can conclude is that a
payment to the person controlling Address B and/or C was made.
Given another transaction from Address C, the picture becomes even
less clear.

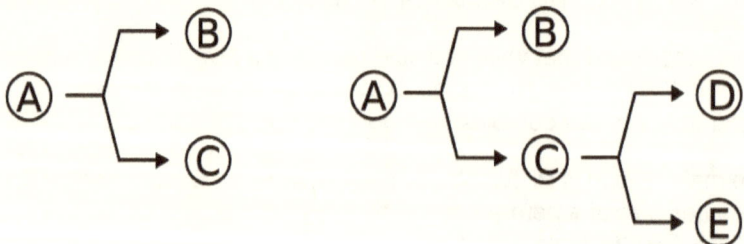

A paid (B **and/or** C)

A paid B **and/or** C;
C paid D **and/or** E

*Change is returned to a one-use address (left). Each
additional payment makes the intended payee more
ambiguous (right).*

An observer trying to link real-world identities to Bitcoin addresses
must gather more secondary information and work harder when all
parties direct change to one-use addresses.

This isn't the end of the story. As transactions generate change,
eventually this change will be recombined to make purchases.
Bringing coins from various change addresses together into a single
transaction suggests (but does not by itself prove) a link to a common

user. Countering this problem requires that additional privacy-enhancing steps be taken. CoinJoin offers one solution, but this is still an area of active research.

STAYING SAFE

Change addresses open the door to loss of funds through several avenues. The most serious problem is that many Bitcoin users are unaware of the existence of change addresses in the first place. However, change addresses can cause problems even for users who understand them.

Discussion forums like the Bitcoin subreddit are filled with stories of users who either lost money or thought they lost money through change addresses. For some specific scenarios based on these stories, and ways to avoid them, see *Five Ways to Lose Money with Bitcoin Change Addresses*.

BACK TO ALICE AND BOB

Given a basic understanding of Bitcoin as a cash system, we can return the the problem of deciding how much of Alice's money will be involved in a payment to Bob.

We have no way to know whether a Alice's wallet contains a coin with a face value of the payment amount (1.05 BTC). As a result, we can't say for sure if this will be the amount of Alice's payment.

Although Alice's address could just happen to contain only one coin, we have no reason to think this is the case, either. For example, her address may contain dozens of coins with face values totaling 2.23 BTC.

To answer the question, we'd need to know the values of each coin at Alice's address. Not only that, but we'd need to know exactly how Alice's wallet selects coins when making payments.

CONCLUSIONS

Like any cash payment, Bitcoin transactions often generate change. This change must be claimed by a change address or lost. The methods that change addresses are created and used lead to important implications for privacy and security. As a Bitcoin user, you owe it to yourself to understand change and how your wallet handles it.

8   BITCOIN SECURITY

Securing bitcoin is challenging because bitcoin is not an abstract reference to value, like a balance in a bank account. Bitcoin is very much like digital cash or gold. You've probably heard the expression, "Possession is nine-tenths of the law." Well, in bitcoin, possession is ten-tenths of the law. Possession of the keys to unlock the bitcoin is equivalent to possession of cash or a chunk of precious metal. You can lose it, misplace it, have it stolen, or accidentally give the wrong amount to someone. In every one of these cases, users have no recourse, just as if they dropped cash on a public sidewalk.

However, bitcoin has capabilities that cash, gold, and bank accounts do not. A bitcoin wallet, containing your keys, can be backed up like any file. It can be stored in multiple copies, even printed on paper for hard-copy backup. You can't "back up" cash, gold, or bank accounts. Bitcoin is different enough from anything that has come before that we need to think about bitcoin security in a novel way too.

SECURITY PRINCIPLES

The core principle in bitcoin is decentralization and it has important implications for security. A centralized model, such as a traditional bank or payment network, depends on access control and vetting to keep bad actors out of the system. By comparison, a decentralized system like bitcoin pushes the responsibility and control to the users.

Because security of the network is based on proof of work, not access control, the network can be open and no encryption is required for bitcoin traffic.

On a traditional payment network, such as a credit card system, the payment is open-ended because it contains the user's private identifier (the credit card number). After the initial charge, anyone with access to the identifier can "pull" funds and charge the owner again and again. Thus, the payment network has to be secured end-to-end with encryption and must ensure that no eavesdroppers or intermediaries can compromise the payment traffic, in transit or when it is stored (at rest). If a bad actor gains access to the system, he can compromise current transactions AND payment tokens that can be used to create new transactions. Worse, when customer data is compromised, the customers are exposed to identity theft and must take action to prevent fraudulent use of the compromised accounts.

Bitcoin is dramatically different. A bitcoin transaction authorizes only a specific value to a specific recipient and cannot be forged or modified. It does not reveal any private information, such as the identities of the parties, and cannot be used to authorize additional payments. Therefore, a bitcoin payment network does not need to be encrypted or protected from eavesdropping. In fact, you can broadcast bitcoin transactions over an open public channel, such as unsecured WiFi or Bluetooth, with no loss of security.

Bitcoin's decentralized security model puts a lot of power in the hands of the users. With that power comes responsibility for maintaining the secrecy of the keys. For most users that is not easy to do, especially on general-purpose computing devices such as Internet-connected smartphones or laptops. Although bitcoin's decentralized model prevents the type of mass compromise seen with credit cards, many users are not able to adequately secure their keys and get hacked, one by one.

8.1.1 DEVELOPING BITCOIN SYSTEMS SECURELY

The most important principle for bitcoin developers is decentralization. Most developers will be familiar with centralized security models and might be tempted to apply these models to their bitcoin applications, with disastrous results.

Bitcoin's security relies on decentralized control over keys and on independent transaction validation by miners. If you want to leverage Bitcoin's security, you need to ensure that you remain within the Bitcoin security model. In simple terms: don't take control of keys away from users and don't take transactions off the blockchain.

For example, many early bitcoin exchanges concentrated all user funds in a single "hot" wallet with keys stored on a single server. Such a design removes control from users and centralizes control over keys in a single system. Many such systems have been hacked, with disastrous consequences for their customers.

Another common mistake is to take transactions "off blockchain" in a misguided effort to reduce transaction fees or accelerate transaction processing. An "off blockchain" system will record transactions on an internal, centralized ledger and only occasionally synchronize them to the bitcoin blockchain. This practice, again, substitutes decentralized bitcoin security with a proprietary and centralized approach. When transactions are off blockchain, improperly secured centralized ledgers can be falsified, diverting funds and depleting reserves, unnoticed.

Unless you are prepared to invest heavily in operational security, multiple layers of access control, and audits (as the traditional banks do) you should think very carefully before taking funds outside of Bitcoin's decentralized security context. Even if you have the funds and discipline to implement a robust security model, such a design merely replicates the fragile model of traditional financial networks, plagued by identity theft, corruption, and embezzlement. To take advantage of Bitcoin's unique decentralized security model, you have to avoid the temptation of centralized architectures that might feel familiar but ultimately subvert Bitcoin's security.

8.1.2 THE ROOT OF TRUST

Traditional security architecture is based upon a concept called the
ROOT OF TRUST, which is a trusted core used as the foundation for
the security of the overall system or application. Security architecture
is developed around the root of trust as a series of concentric circles,
like layers in an onion, extending trust outward from the center. Each
layer builds upon the more-trusted inner layer using access controls,
digital signatures, encryption, and other security primitives. As
software systems become more complex, they are more likely to
contain bugs, which make them vulnerable to security compromise.
As a result, the more complex a software system becomes, the harder
it is to secure. The root of trust concept ensures that most of the trust
is placed within the least complex part of the system, and therefore
least vulnerable, parts of the system, while more complex software is
layered around it. This security architecture is repeated at different
scales, first establishing a root of trust within the hardware of a single
system, then extending that root of trust through the operating system
to higher-level system services, and finally across many servers
layered in concentric circles of diminishing trust.

Bitcoin security architecture is different. In Bitcoin, the consensus
system creates a trusted public ledger that is completely
decentralized. A correctly validated blockchain uses the genesis block
as the root of trust, building a chain of trust up to the current block.
Bitcoin systems can and should use the blockchain as their root of
trust. When designing a complex bitcoin application that consists of
services on many different systems, you should carefully examine the
security architecture in order to ascertain where trust is being placed.
Ultimately, the only thing that should be explicitly trusted is a fully
validated blockchain. If your application explicitly or implicitly vests
trust in anything but the blockchain, that should be a source of
concern because it introduces vulnerability. A good method to
evaluate the security architecture of your application is to consider
each individual component and evaluate a hypothetical scenario
where that component is completely compromised and under the
control of a malicious actor. Take each component of your application,
in turn, and assess the impacts on the overall security if that

component is compromised. If your application is no longer secure when components are compromised, that shows you have misplaced trust in those components. A bitcoin application without vulnerabilities should be vulnerable only to a compromise of the bitcoin consensus mechanism, meaning that its root of trust is based on the strongest part of the bitcoin security architecture.

The numerous examples of hacked bitcoin exchanges serve to underscore this point because their security architecture and design fails even under the most casual scrutiny. These centralized implementations had invested trust explicitly in numerous components outside the bitcoin blockchain, such as hot wallets, centralized ledger databases, vulnerable encryption keys, and similar schemes.

USER SECURITY BEST PRACTICES

Humans have used physical security controls for thousands of years. By comparison, our experience with digital security is less than 50 years old. Modern general-purpose operating systems are not very secure and not particularly suited to storing digital money. Our computers are constantly exposed to external threats via always-on Internet connections. They run thousands of software components from hundreds of authors, often with unconstrained access to the user's files. A single piece of rogue software, among the many thousands installed on your computer, can compromise your keyboard and files, stealing any bitcoin stored in wallet applications. The level of computer maintenance required to keep a computer virus-free and trojan-free is beyond the skill level of all but a tiny minority of computer users.

Despite decades of research and advancements in information security, digital assets are still woefully vulnerable to a determined adversary. Even the most highly protected and restricted systems, in financial services companies, intelligence agencies, and defense contractors, are frequently breached. Bitcoin creates digital assets that have intrinsic value and can be stolen and diverted to new owners instantly and irrevocably. This creates a massive incentive for hackers. Until now, hackers had to convert identity information or account tokens—such as credit cards, and bank accounts—into value after compromising them. Despite the difficulty of fencing and laundering financial information, we have seen ever-escalating thefts. Bitcoin escalates this problem because it doesn't need to be fenced or laundered; it is intrinsic value within a digital asset.

Fortunately, bitcoin also creates the incentives to improve computer security. Whereas previously the risk of computer compromise was vague and indirect, bitcoin makes these risks clear and obvious. Holding bitcoin on a computer serves to focus the user's mind on the need for improved computer security. As a direct result of the proliferation and increased adoption of bitcoin and other digital currencies, we have seen an escalation in both hacking techniques and security solutions. In simple terms, hackers now have a very juicy target and users have a clear incentive to defend themselves.

Over the past three years, as a direct result of bitcoin adoption, we have seen tremendous innovation in the realm of information security in the form of hardware encryption, key storage and hardware wallets, multi-signature technology, and digital escrow. In the following sections we will examine various best practices for practical user security.

8.1.3 PHYSICAL BITCOIN STORAGE

Because most users are far more comfortable with physical security than information security, a very effective method for protecting bitcoins is to convert them into physical form. Bitcoin keys are nothing more than long numbers. This means that they can be stored in a physical form, such as printed on paper or etched on a metal coin. Securing the keys then becomes as simple as physically securing the printed copy of the bitcoin keys. A set of bitcoin keys that is printed on paper is called a "paper wallet," and there are many free tools that can be used to create them. I personally keep the vast majority of my bitcoins (99% or more) stored on paper wallets, encrypted with BIP0038, with multiple copies locked in safes. Keeping bitcoin offline is called COLD STORAGE and it is one of the most effective security techniques. A cold storage system is one where the keys are generated on an offline system (one never connected to the Internet) and stored offline either on paper or on digital media, such as a USB memory stick.

8.1.4 HARDWARE WALLETS

In the long term, bitcoin security increasingly will take the form of hardware tamper-proof wallets. Unlike a smartphone or desktop computer, a bitcoin hardware wallet has just one purpose: to hold bitcoins securely. Without general-purpose software to compromise and with limited interfaces, hardware wallets can deliver an almost foolproof level of security to nonexpert users. I expect to see hardware wallets become the predominant method of bitcoin storage. For an example of such a hardware wallet, see the Trezor.

8.1.5 BALANCING RISK

Although most users are rightly concerned about bitcoin theft, there is an even bigger risk. Data files get lost all the time. If they contain bitcoin, the loss is much more painful. In the effort to secure their bitcoin wallets, users must be very careful not to go too far and end up losing the bitcoin. In July of 2011, a well-known bitcoin awareness and education project lost almost 7,000 bitcoins. In their effort to prevent theft, the owners had implemented a complex series of encrypted backups. In the end they accidentally lost the encryption keys, making the backups worthless and losing a fortune. Like hiding money by burying it in the desert, if you secure your bitcoin too well you might not be able to find it again.

8.1.6 DIVERSIFYING RISK

Would you carry your entire net worth in cash in your wallet? Most people would consider that reckless, yet bitcoin users often keep all their bitcoin in a single wallet. Instead, users should spread the risk among multiple and diverse bitcoin wallets. Prudent users will keep only a small fraction, perhaps less than 5%, of their bitcoins in an online or mobile wallet as "pocket change." The rest should be split between a few different storage mechanisms, such as a desktop wallet and offline (cold storage).

8.1.7 MULTI-SIG AND GOVERNANCE

Whenever a company or individual stores large amounts of bitcoin, they should consider using a multi-signature bitcoin address. Multi-signature addresses secure funds by requiring more than one signature to make a payment. The signing keys should be stored in a number of different locations and under the control of different people. In a corporate environment, for example, the keys should be generated independently and held by several company executives, to ensure no single person can compromise the funds. Multi-signature addresses can also offer redundancy, where a single person holds several keys that are stored in different locations.

8.1.8 SURVIVABILITY

One important security consideration that is often overlooked is availability, especially in the context of incapacity or death of the key holder. Bitcoin users are told to use complex passwords and keep their keys secure and private, not sharing them with anyone. Unfortunately, that practice makes it almost impossible for the user's family to recover any funds if the user is not available to unlock them. In most cases, in fact, the families of bitcoin users might be completely unaware of the existence of the bitcoin funds.

If you have a lot of bitcoin, you should consider sharing access details with a trusted relative or lawyer. A more complex survivability scheme can be set up with multi-signature access and estate planning through a lawyer specialized as a "digital asset executor."

8.1.9 CONCLUSION

Bitcoin is a completely new, unprecedented, and complex technology. Over time we will develop better security tools and practices that are easier to use by nonexperts. For now, bitcoin users can use many of the tips discussed here to enjoy a secure and trouble-free bitcoin experience.

9 FREQUENTLY ASKED QUESTIONS

9.1.1 WHAT IS BITCOIN?

Bitcoin is a consensus network that enables a new payment system and a completely digital money. It is the first decentralized peer-to-peer payment network that is powered by its users with no central authority or middlemen. From a user perspective, Bitcoin is pretty much like cash for the Internet. Bitcoin can also be seen as the most prominent triple entry bookkeeping system in existence.

9.1.2 WHO CREATED BITCOIN?

Bitcoin is the first implementation of a concept called "cryptocurrency", which was first described in 1998 by Wei Dai on the cypherpunks mailing list, suggesting the idea of a new form of money that uses cryptography to control its creation and transactions, rather than a central authority. The first Bitcoin specification, and proof of concept was published in 2009 in a cryptography mailing list by Satoshi Nakamoto. Satoshi left the project in late 2010 without revealing much about himself. The community has since grown exponentially with many developers working on Bitcoin.

Satoshi's anonymity often raised unjustified concerns, many of which are linked to misunderstanding of the open-source nature of Bitcoin.

The Bitcoin protocol and software are published openly and any developer around the world can review the code or make their own modified version of the Bitcoin software. Just like current developers, Satoshi's influence was limited to the changes he made being adopted by others and therefore he did not control Bitcoin. As such, the identity of Bitcoin's inventor is probably as relevant today as the identity of the person who invented paper.

9.1.3 WHO CONTROLS THE BITCOIN NETWORK?

Nobody owns the Bitcoin network much like no one owns the technology behind email. Bitcoin is controlled by all Bitcoin users around the world. While developers are improving the software, they can't force a change in the Bitcoin protocol because all users are free to choose what software and version they use. In order to stay compatible with each other, all users need to use software complying with the same rules. Bitcoin can only work correctly with a complete consensus among all users. Therefore, all users and developers have a strong incentive to protect this consensus.

9.1.4 HOW DOES BITCOIN WORK?

From a user perspective, Bitcoin is nothing more than a mobile app or computer program that provides a personal Bitcoin wallet and allows a user to send and receive bitcoins with them. This is how Bitcoin works for most users.

Behind the scenes, the Bitcoin network is sharing a public ledger called the "block chain". This ledger contains every transaction ever processed, allowing a user's computer to verify the validity of each transaction. The authenticity of each transaction is protected by digital signatures corresponding to the sending addresses, allowing all users to have full control over sending bitcoins from their own Bitcoin addresses. In addition, anyone can process transactions using the computing power of specialized hardware and earn a reward in bitcoins for this service. This is often called "mining". To learn more about Bitcoin, you can consult the dedicated page and the original paper.

9.1.5 IS BITCOIN REALLY USED BY PEOPLE?

Yes. There is a growing number of businesses and individuals using Bitcoin. This includes brick and mortar businesses like restaurants, apartments, law firms, and popular online services such as Namecheap, WordPress, and Reddit. While Bitcoin remains a relatively new phenomenon, it is growing fast. At the end of August 2015, the value of all bitcoins in circulation exceeded US$ 3.1 billion with millions of dollars worth of bitcoins exchanged daily.

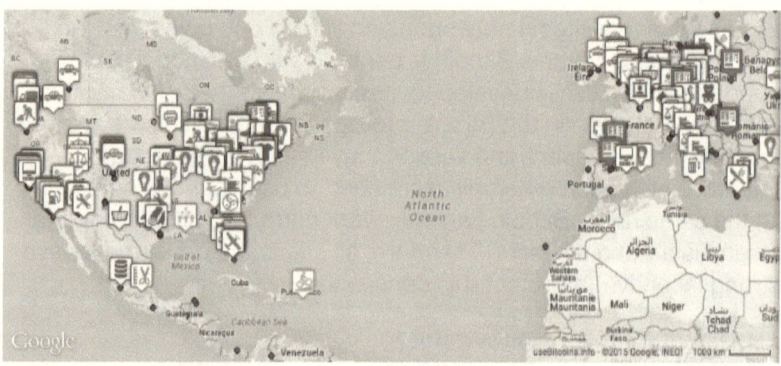

9.1.6 HOW DOES ONE ACQUIRE BITCOINS?

- As payment for goods or services.
- Purchase bitcoins at a Bitcoin exchange.
- Exchange bitcoins with someone near you.
- Earn bitcoins through competitive mining.

While it may be possible to find individuals who wish to sell bitcoins in exchange for a credit card or PayPal payment, most exchanges do not allow funding via these payment methods. This is due to cases where someone buys bitcoins with PayPal, and then reverses their half of the transaction. This is commonly referred to as a chargeback.

9.1.7 HOW DIFFICULT IS IT TO MAKE A BITCOIN PAYMENT?

Bitcoin payments are easier to make than debit or credit card purchases, and can be received without a merchant account.

Payments are made from a wallet application, either on your computer or smartphone, by entering the recipient's address, the payment amount, and pressing send. To make it easier to enter a recipient's address, many wallets can obtain the address by scanning a QR code or touching two phones together with NFC technology.

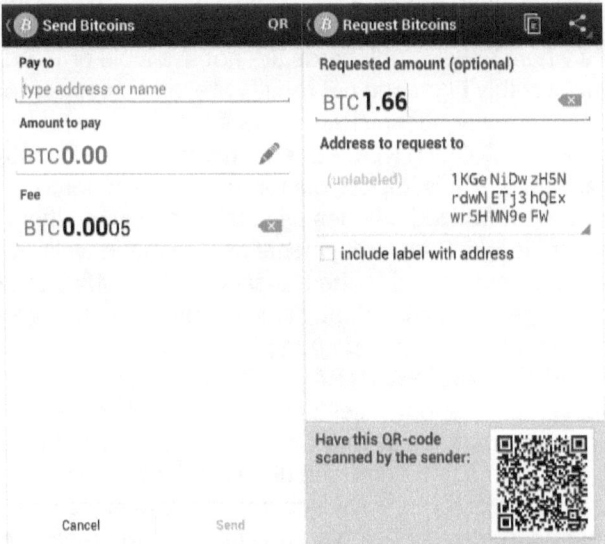

9.1.8 WHAT ARE THE ADVANTAGES OF BITCOIN?

- **PAYMENT FREEDOM** - It is possible to send and receive any amount of money instantly anywhere in the world at any time. No bank holidays. No borders. No imposed limits. Bitcoin allows its users to be in full control of their money.
- **VERY LOW FEES** - Bitcoin payments are currently processed with either no fees or extremely small fees. Users may include fees with transactions to receive priority processing, which results in faster confirmation of transactions by the network. Additionally, merchant processors exist to assist merchants in processing transactions, converting bitcoins to fiat currency and depositing funds directly into merchants' bank accounts daily.

As these services are based on Bitcoin, they can be offered for much lower fees than with PayPal or credit card networks.

- **FEWER RISKS FOR MERCHANTS** - Bitcoin transactions are secure, irreversible, and do not contain customers' sensitive or personal information. This protects merchants from losses caused by fraud or fraudulent chargebacks, and there is no need for PCI compliance. Merchants can easily expand to new markets where either credit cards are not available or fraud rates are unacceptably high. The net results are lower fees, larger markets, and fewer administrative costs.
- **SECURITY AND CONTROL** - Bitcoin users are in full control of their transactions; it is impossible for merchants to force unwanted or unnoticed charges as can happen with other payment methods. Bitcoin payments can be made without personal information tied to the transaction. This offers strong protection against identity theft. Bitcoin users can also protect their money with backup and encryption.
- **TRANSPARENT AND NEUTRAL** - All information concerning the Bitcoin money supply itself is readily available on the block chain for anybody to verify and use in real-time. No individual or organization can control or manipulate the Bitcoin protocol because it is cryptographically secure. This allows the core of Bitcoin to be trusted for being completely neutral, transparent and predictable.

9.1.9 WHAT ARE THE DISADVANTAGES OF BITCOIN?

- **DEGREE OF ACCEPTANCE** - Many people are still unaware of Bitcoin. Every day, more businesses accept bitcoins because they want the advantages of doing so, but the list remains small and still needs to grow in order to benefit from network effects.
- **VOLATILITY** - The total value of bitcoins in circulation and the number of businesses using Bitcoin are still very small compared to what they could be. Therefore, relatively small events, trades, or business activities can significantly affect the price. In theory, this volatility will decrease as Bitcoin markets and the technology matures. Never before has the world seen a start-up

currency, so it is truly difficult (and exciting) to imagine how it will play out.

- **ONGOING DEVELOPMENT** - Bitcoin software is still in beta with many incomplete features in active development. New tools, features, and services are being developed to make Bitcoin more secure and accessible to the masses. Some of these are still not ready for everyone. Most Bitcoin businesses are new and still offer no insurance. In general, Bitcoin is still in the process of maturing.

9.1.10   WHY DO PEOPLE TRUST BITCOIN?

Much of the trust in Bitcoin comes from the fact that it requires no trust at all. Bitcoin is fully open-source and decentralized. This means that anyone has access to the entire source code at any time. Any developer in the world can therefore verify exactly how Bitcoin works. All transactions and bitcoins issued into existence can be transparently consulted in real-time by anyone. All payments can be made without reliance on a third party and the whole system is protected by heavily peer-reviewed cryptographic algorithms, like those used for online banking. No organization or individual can control Bitcoin, and the network remains secure even if not all of its users can be trusted.

9.1.11   CAN I MAKE MONEY WITH BITCOIN?

You should never expect to get rich with Bitcoin or any emerging technology. It is always important to be wary of anything that sounds too good to be true or disobeys basic economic rules.

Bitcoin is a growing space of innovation and there are business opportunities that also include risks. There is no guarantee that Bitcoin will continue to grow even though it has developed at a very fast rate so far. Investing time and resources on anything related to Bitcoin requires entrepreneurship. There are various ways to make money with Bitcoin such as mining, speculation or running new businesses. All of these methods are competitive and there is no guarantee of profit. It is up to each individual to make a proper evaluation of the costs and the risks involved in any such project.

9.1.12   IS BITCOIN FULLY VIRTUAL AND IMMATERIAL?

Bitcoin is as virtual as the credit cards and online banking networks people use everyday. Bitcoin can be used to pay online and in physical stores just like any other form of money. Bitcoins can also be exchanged in physical form such as the Casascius coins, but paying with a mobile phone usually remains more convenient. Bitcoin balances are stored in a large distributed network, and they cannot be fraudulently altered by anybody. In other words, Bitcoin users have exclusive control over their funds and bitcoins cannot vanish just because they are virtual.

9.1.13   IS BITCOIN ANONYMOUS?

Bitcoin is designed to allow its users to send and receive payments with an acceptable level of privacy as well as any other form of money. However, Bitcoin is not anonymous and cannot offer the same level of privacy as cash. The use of Bitcoin leaves extensive public records. Various mechanisms exist to protect users' privacy, and more are in development. However, there is still work to be done before these features are used correctly by most Bitcoin users.

Some concerns have been raised that private transactions could be used for illegal purposes with Bitcoin. However, it is worth noting that Bitcoin will undoubtedly be subjected to similar regulations that are already in place inside existing financial systems. Bitcoin cannot be more anonymous than cash and it is not likely to prevent criminal investigations from being conducted. Additionally, Bitcoin is also designed to prevent a large range of financial crimes.

9.1.14   WHAT HAPPENS WHEN BITCOINS ARE LOST?

When a user loses his wallet, it has the effect of removing money out of circulation. Lost bitcoins still remain in the block chain just like any other bitcoins. However, lost bitcoins remain dormant forever because there is no way for anybody to find the private key(s) that would allow them to be spent again. Because of the law of supply and demand, when fewer bitcoins are available, the ones that are left will be in higher demand and increase in value to compensate.

9.1.15 CAN BITCOIN SCALE TO BECOME A MAJOR PAYMENT NETWORK?

The Bitcoin network can already process a much higher number of transactions per second than it does today. It is, however, not entirely ready to scale to the level of major credit card networks. Work is underway to lift current limitations, and future requirements are well known. Since inception, every aspect of the Bitcoin network has been in a continuous process of maturation, optimization, and specialization, and it should be expected to remain that way for some years to come. As traffic grows, more Bitcoin users may use lightweight clients, and full network nodes may become a more specialized service. For more details, see the Scalability page on the Wiki.

LEGAL

9.1.16 IS BITCOIN LEGAL?

To the best of our knowledge, Bitcoin has not been made illegal by legislation in most jurisdictions. However, some jurisdictions (such as Argentina and Russia) severely restrict or ban foreign currencies. Other jurisdictions (such as Thailand) may limit the licensing of certain entities such as Bitcoin exchanges.

Regulators from various jurisdictions are taking steps to provide individuals and businesses with rules on how to integrate this new technology with the formal, regulated financial system. For example, the Financial Crimes Enforcement Network (FinCEN), a bureau in the United States Treasury Department, issued non binding guidance on how it characterizes certain activities involving virtual currencies.

9.1.17 IS BITCOIN USEFUL FOR ILLEGAL ACTIVITIES?

Bitcoin is money, and money has always been used both for legal and illegal purposes. Cash, credit cards and current banking systems widely surpass Bitcoin in terms of their use to finance crime. Bitcoin can bring significant innovation in payment systems and the benefits of such innovation are often considered to be far beyond their potential drawbacks.

Bitcoin is designed to be a huge step forward in making money more secure and could also act as a significant protection against many forms of financial crime. For instance, bitcoins are completely impossible to counterfeit. Users are in full control of their payments and cannot receive unapproved charges such as with credit card fraud. Bitcoin transactions are irreversible and immune to fraudulent chargebacks. Bitcoin allows money to be secured against theft and loss using very strong and useful mechanisms such as backups, encryption, and multiple signatures.

Some concerns have been raised that Bitcoin could be more attractive to criminals because it can be used to make private and irreversible payments. However, these features already exist with cash and wire transfer, which are widely used and well-established. The use of Bitcoin will undoubtedly be subjected to similar regulations that are already in place inside existing financial systems, and Bitcoin is not likely to prevent criminal investigations from being conducted. In general, it is common for important breakthroughs to be perceived as being controversial before their benefits are well understood. The Internet is a good example among many others to illustrate this.

9.1.18 CAN BITCOIN BE REGULATED?

The Bitcoin protocol itself cannot be modified without the cooperation of nearly all its users, who choose what software they use. Attempting to assign special rights to a local authority in the rules of the global Bitcoin network is not a practical possibility. Any rich organization could choose to invest in mining hardware to control half of the computing power of the network and become able to block or reverse recent transactions. However, there is no guarantee that they could retain this power since this requires to invest as much than all other miners in the world.

It is however possible to regulate the use of Bitcoin in a similar way to any other instrument. Just like the dollar, Bitcoin can be used for a wide variety of purposes, some of which can be considered legitimate or not as per each jurisdiction's laws. In this regard, Bitcoin is no different than any other tool or resource and can be subjected to different regulations in each country. Bitcoin use could also be made difficult by restrictive regulations, in which case it is hard to determine what percentage of users would keep using the technology. A government that chooses to ban Bitcoin would prevent domestic businesses and markets from developing, shifting innovation to other countries. The challenge for regulators, as always, is to develop efficient solutions while not impairing the growth of new emerging markets and businesses.

9.1.19   WHAT ABOUT BITCOIN AND TAXES?

Bitcoin is not a fiat currency with legal tender status in any jurisdiction, but often tax liability accrues regardless of the medium used. There is a wide variety of legislation in many different jurisdictions which could cause income, sales, payroll, capital gains, or some other form of tax liability to arise with Bitcoin.

9.1.20   WHAT ABOUT BITCOIN AND CONSUMER PROTECTION?

Bitcoin is freeing people to transact on their own terms. Each user can send and receive payments in a similar way to cash but they can also take part in more complex contracts. Multiple signatures allow a transaction to be accepted by the network only if a certain number of a defined group of persons agree to sign the transaction. This allows innovative dispute mediation services to be developed in the future. Such services could allow a third party to approve or reject a transaction in case of disagreement between the other parties without having control on their money. As opposed to cash and other payment methods, Bitcoin always leaves a public proof that a transaction did take place, which can potentially be used in a recourse against businesses with fraudulent practices.

It is also worth noting that while merchants usually depend on their public reputation to remain in business and pay their employees, they don't have access to the same level of information when dealing with new consumers. The way Bitcoin works allows both individuals and businesses to be protected against fraudulent chargebacks while giving the choice to the consumer to ask for more protection when they are not willing to trust a particular merchant.

ECONOMY

9.1.21   HOW ARE BITCOINS CREATED?

New bitcoins are generated by a competitive and decentralized process called "mining". This process involves that individuals are rewarded by the network for their services. Bitcoin miners are processing transactions and securing the network using specialized hardware and are collecting new bitcoins in exchange.

The Bitcoin protocol is designed in such a way that new bitcoins are created at a fixed rate. This makes Bitcoin mining a very competitive business. When more miners join the network, it becomes increasingly difficult to make a profit and miners must seek efficiency to cut their operating costs. No central authority or developer has any power to control or manipulate the system to increase their profits. Every Bitcoin node in the world will reject anything that does not comply with the rules it expects the system to follow.

Bitcoins are created at a decreasing and predictable rate. The number of new bitcoins created each year is automatically halved over time until bitcoin issuance halts completely with a total of 21 million bitcoins in existence. At this point, Bitcoin miners will probably be supported exclusively by numerous small transaction fees.

9.1.22   WHY DO BITCOINS HAVE VALUE?

Bitcoins have value because they are useful as a form of money. Bitcoin has the characteristics of money (durability, portability, fungibility, scarcity, divisibility, and recognizability) based on the properties of mathematics rather than relying on physical properties (like gold and silver) or trust in central authorities (like fiat currencies). In short, Bitcoin is backed by mathematics. With these attributes, all that is required for a form of money to hold value is trust and adoption. In the case of Bitcoin, this can be measured by its growing base of users, merchants, and startups. As with all currency, bitcoin's value comes only and directly from people willing to accept them as payment.

9.1.23 WHAT DETERMINES BITCOIN'S PRICE?

The price of a bitcoin is determined by supply and demand. When demand for bitcoins increases, the price increases, and when demand falls, the price falls. There is only a limited number of bitcoins in circulation and new bitcoins are created at a predictable and decreasing rate, which means that demand must follow this level of inflation to keep the price stable. Because Bitcoin is still a relatively small market compared to what it could be, it doesn't take significant amounts of money to move the market price up or down, and thus the price of a bitcoin is still very volatile.

Bitcoin price over time:

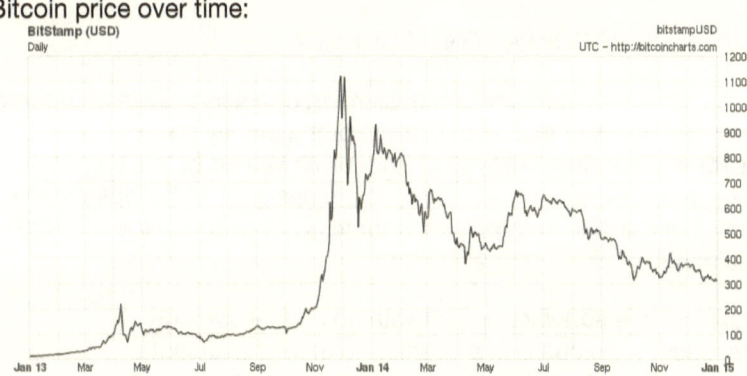

9.1.24 CAN BITCOINS BECOME WORTHLESS?

Yes. History is littered with currencies that failed and are no longer used, such as the German Mark during the Weimar Republic and, more recently, the Zimbabwean dollar. Although previous currency failures were typically due to hyperinflation of a kind that Bitcoin makes impossible, there is always potential for technical failures, competing currencies, political issues and so on. As a basic rule of thumb, no currency should be considered absolutely safe from failures or hard times. Bitcoin has proven reliable for years since its inception and there is a lot of potential for Bitcoin to continue to grow. However, no one is in a position to predict what the future will be for Bitcoin.

9.1.25   IS BITCOIN A BUBBLE?

A fast rise in price does not constitute a bubble. An artificial over-valuation that will lead to a sudden downward correction constitutes a bubble. Choices based on individual human action by hundreds of thousands of market participants is the cause for bitcoin's price to fluctuate as the market seeks price discovery. Reasons for changes in sentiment may include a loss of confidence in Bitcoin, a large difference between value and price not based on the fundamentals of the Bitcoin economy, increased press coverage stimulating speculative demand, fear of uncertainty, and old-fashioned irrational exuberance and greed.

9.1.26   IS BITCOIN A PONZI SCHEME?

A Ponzi scheme is a fraudulent investment operation that pays returns to its investors from their own money, or the money paid by subsequent investors, instead of from profit earned by the individuals running the business. Ponzi schemes are designed to collapse at the expense of the last investors when there is not enough new participants.

Bitcoin is a free software project with no central authority. Consequently, no one is in a position to make fraudulent representations about investment returns. Like other major currencies such as gold, United States dollar, euro, yen, etc. there is no guaranteed purchasing power and the exchange rate floats freely. This leads to volatility where owners of bitcoins can unpredictably make or lose money. Beyond speculation, Bitcoin is also a payment system with useful and competitive attributes that are being used by thousands of users and businesses.

9.1.27 DOESN'T BITCOIN UNFAIRLY BENEFIT EARLY ADOPTERS?

Some early adopters have large numbers of bitcoins because they took risks and invested time and resources in an unproven technology that was hardly used by anyone and that was much harder to secure properly. Many early adopters spent large numbers of bitcoins quite a few times before they became valuable or bought only small amounts and didn't make huge gains. There is no guarantee that the price of a bitcoin will increase or drop. This is very similar to investing in an early startup that can either gain value through its usefulness and popularity, or just never break through. Bitcoin is still in its infancy, and it has been designed with a very long-term view; it is hard to imagine how it could be less biased towards early adopters, and today's users may or may not be the early adopters of tomorrow.

9.1.28 WON'T THE FINITE AMOUNT OF BITCOINS BE A LIMITATION?

Bitcoin is unique in that only 21 million bitcoins will ever be created. However, this will never be a limitation because transactions can be denominated in smaller sub-units of a bitcoin, such as bits - there are 1,000,000 bits in 1 bitcoin. Bitcoins can be divided up to 8 decimal places (0.000 000 01) and potentially even smaller units if that is ever required in the future as the average transaction size decreases.

9.1.29 WON'T BITCOIN FALL IN A DEFLATIONARY SPIRAL?

The deflationary spiral theory says that if prices are expected to fall, people will move purchases into the future in order to benefit from the lower prices. That fall in demand will in turn cause merchants to lower their prices to try and stimulate demand, making the problem worse and leading to an economic depression.

Although this theory is a popular way to justify inflation amongst central bankers, it does not appear to always hold true and is considered controversial amongst economists. Consumer electronics is one example of a market where prices constantly fall but which is not in depression. Similarly, the value of bitcoins has risen over time and yet the size of the Bitcoin economy has also grown dramatically along with it. Because both the value of the currency and the size of its economy started at zero in 2009, Bitcoin is a counterexample to the theory showing that it must sometimes be wrong.

Notwithstanding this, Bitcoin is not designed to be a deflationary currency. It is more accurate to say Bitcoin is intended to inflate in its early years, and become stable in its later years. The only time the quantity of bitcoins in circulation will drop is if people carelessly lose their wallets by failing to make backups. With a stable monetary base and a stable economy, the value of the currency should remain the same.

9.1.30   ISN'T SPECULATION AND VOLATILITY A PROBLEM FOR BITCOIN?

This is a chicken and egg situation. For bitcoin's price to stabilize, a large scale economy needs to develop with more businesses and users. For a large scale economy to develop, businesses and users will seek for price stability.

Fortunately, volatility does not affect the main benefits of Bitcoin as a payment system to transfer money from point A to point B. It is possible for businesses to convert bitcoin payments to their local currency instantly, allowing them to profit from the advantages of Bitcoin without being subjected to price fluctuations. Since Bitcoin offers many useful and unique features and properties, many users choose to use Bitcoin. With such solutions and incentives, it is possible that Bitcoin will mature and develop to a degree where price volatility will become limited.

9.1.31   WHAT IF SOMEONE BOUGHT UP ALL THE EXISTING BITCOINS?

Only a fraction of bitcoins issued to date are found on the exchange markets for sale. Bitcoin markets are competitive, meaning the price of a bitcoin will rise or fall depending on supply and demand. Additionally, new bitcoins will continue to be issued for decades to come. Therefore even the most determined buyer could not buy all the bitcoins in existence. This situation isn't to suggest, however, that the markets aren't vulnerable to price manipulation; it still doesn't take significant amounts of money to move the market price up or down, and thus Bitcoin remains a volatile asset thus far.

9.1.32   WHAT IF SOMEONE CREATES A BETTER DIGITAL CURRENCY?

That can happen. For now, Bitcoin remains by far the most popular decentralized virtual currency, but there can be no guarantee that it will retain that position. There is already a set of alternative currencies inspired by Bitcoin. It is however probably correct to assume that significant improvements would be required for a new currency to overtake Bitcoin in terms of established market, even though this remains unpredictable. Bitcoin could also conceivably adopt improvements of a competing currency so long as it doesn't change fundamental parts of the protocol.

TRANSACTIONS

9.1.33   WHY DO I HAVE TO WAIT 10 MINUTES?

Receiving a payment is almost instant with Bitcoin. However, there is a 10 minutes delay on average before the network begins to confirm your transaction by including it in a block and before you can spend the bitcoins you receive. A confirmation means that there is a consensus on the network that the bitcoins you received haven't been sent to anyone else and are considered your property. Once your transaction has been included in one block, it will continue to be buried under every block after it, which will exponentially consolidate this consensus and decrease the risk of a reversed transaction. Every user is free to determine at what point they consider a transaction confirmed, but 6 confirmations is often considered to be as safe as waiting 6 months on a credit card transaction.

9.1.34   HOW MUCH WILL THE TRANSACTION FEE BE?

Most transactions can be processed without fees, but users are encouraged to pay a small voluntary fee for faster confirmation of their transactions and to remunerate miners. When fees are required, they generally don't exceed a few pennies in value. Your Bitcoin client will usually try to estimate an appropriate fee when required.

Transaction fees are used as a protection against users sending transactions to overload the network. The precise manner in which fees work is still being developed and will change over time. Because the fee is not related to the amount of bitcoins being sent, it may seem extremely low (0.0005 BTC for a 1,000 BTC transfer) or unfairly high (0.004 BTC for a 0.02 BTC payment). The fee is defined by attributes such as data in transaction and transaction recurrence. For example, if you are receiving a large number of tiny amounts, then fees for sending will be higher. Such payments are comparable to paying a restaurant bill using only pennies. Spending small fractions of your bitcoins rapidly may also require a fee. If your activity follows the pattern of conventional transactions, the fees should remain very low.

9.1.35   WHAT IF I RECEIVE A BITCOIN WHEN MY COMPUTER IS POWERED OFF?

This works fine. The bitcoins will appear next time you start your wallet application. Bitcoins are not actually received by the software on your computer, they are appended to a public ledger that is shared between all the devices on the network. If you are sent bitcoins when your wallet client program is not running and you later launch it, it will download blocks and catch up with any transactions it did not already know about, and the bitcoins will eventually appear as if they were just received in real time. Your wallet is only needed when you wish to spend bitcoins.

9.1.36   WHAT DOES "SYNCHRONIZING" MEAN AND WHY DOES IT TAKE SO LONG?

Long synchronization time is only required with full node clients like Bitcoin Core. Technically speaking, synchronizing is the process of downloading and verifying all previous Bitcoin transactions on the network. For some Bitcoin clients to calculate the spendable balance of your Bitcoin wallet and make new transactions, it needs to be aware of all previous transactions. This step can be resource intensive and requires sufficient bandwidth and storage to accommodate the full size of the block chain. For Bitcoin to remain secure, enough people should keep using full node clients because they perform the task of validating and relaying transactions.

MINING

9.1.37   WHAT IS BITCOIN MINING?

Mining is the process of spending computing power to process transactions, secure the network, and keep everyone in the system synchronized together. It can be perceived like the Bitcoin data center except that it has been designed to be fully decentralized with miners operating in all countries and no individual having control over the network. This process is referred to as "mining" as an analogy to gold mining because it is also a temporary mechanism used to issue new bitcoins. Unlike gold mining, however, Bitcoin mining provides a reward in exchange for useful services required to operate a secure payment network. Mining will still be required after the last bitcoin is issued.

9.1.38   HOW DOES BITCOIN MINING WORK?

Anybody can become a Bitcoin miner by running software with specialized hardware. Mining software listens for transactions broadcast through the peer-to-peer network and performs appropriate tasks to process and confirm these transactions. Bitcoin miners perform this work because they can earn transaction fees paid by users for faster transaction processing, and newly created bitcoins issued into existence according to a fixed formula.

For new transactions to be confirmed, they need to be included in a block along with a mathematical proof of work. Such proofs are very hard to generate because there is no way to create them other than by trying billions of calculations per second. This requires miners to perform these calculations before their blocks are accepted by the network and before they are rewarded. As more people start to mine, the difficulty of finding valid blocks is automatically increased by the network. This is to ensure that the average time to find a block remains equal to 10 minutes. As a result, mining is a very competitive business where no individual miner can control what is included in the block chain.

The proof of work is also designed to depend on the previous block to force a chronological order in the block chain. This makes it exponentially difficult to reverse previous transactions because this requires the recalculation of the proofs of work of all the subsequent blocks. When two blocks are found at the same time, miners work on the first block they receive and switch to the longest chain of blocks as soon as the next block is found. This allows mining to secure and maintain a global consensus based on processing power.

Bitcoin miners are neither able to cheat by increasing their own reward nor process fraudulent transactions that could corrupt the Bitcoin network because all Bitcoin nodes would reject any block that contains invalid data as per the rules of the Bitcoin protocol. Consequently, the network remains secure even if not all Bitcoin miners can be trusted.

9.1.39   ISN'T BITCOIN MINING A WASTE OF ENERGY?

Spending energy to secure and operate a payment system is hardly a waste. Like any other payment service, the use of Bitcoin entails processing costs. Services necessary for the operation of currently widespread monetary systems, such as banks, credit cards, and armored vehicles, also use a lot of energy. Although unlike Bitcoin, their total energy consumption is not transparent and cannot be as easily measured.

Bitcoin mining has been designed to become more optimized over time with specialized hardware consuming less energy, and the operating costs of mining should continue to be proportional to demand. When Bitcoin mining becomes too competitive and less profitable, some miners choose to stop their activities. Furthermore, all energy expended mining is eventually transformed into heat, and the most profitable miners will be those who have put this heat to good use. An optimally efficient mining network is one that isn't actually consuming any extra energy. While this is an ideal, the economics of mining are such that miners individually strive toward it.

9.1.40   HOW DOES MINING HELP SECURE BITCOIN?

Mining creates the equivalent of a competitive lottery that makes it very difficult for anyone to consecutively add new blocks of transactions into the block chain. This protects the neutrality of the network by preventing any individual from gaining the power to block certain transactions. This also prevents any individual from replacing parts of the block chain to roll back their own spends, which could be used to defraud other users. Mining makes it exponentially more difficult to reverse a past transaction by requiring the rewriting of all blocks following this transaction.

9.1.41   WHAT DO I NEED TO START MINING?

In the early days of Bitcoin, anyone could find a new block using their computer's CPU. As more and more people started mining, the difficulty of finding new blocks increased greatly to the point where the only cost-effective method of mining today is using specialized hardware. You can visit BitcoinMining.com for more information.

SECURITY

9.1.42   IS BITCOIN SECURE?

The Bitcoin technology - the protocol and the cryptography - has a strong security track record, and the Bitcoin network is probably the biggest distributed computing project in the world. Bitcoin's most common vulnerability is in user error. Bitcoin wallet files that store the necessary private keys can be accidentally deleted, lost or stolen. This is pretty similar to physical cash stored in a digital form. Fortunately, users can employ sound security practices to protect their money or use service providers that offer good levels of security and insurance against theft or loss.

9.1.43   HASN'T BITCOIN BEEN HACKED IN THE PAST?

The rules of the protocol and the cryptography used for Bitcoin are still working years after its inception, which is a good indication that the concept is well designed. However, security flaws have been found and fixed over time in various software implementations. Like any other form of software, the security of Bitcoin software depends on the speed with which problems are found and fixed. The more such issues are discovered, the more Bitcoin is gaining maturity.

There are often misconceptions about thefts and security breaches that happened on diverse exchanges and businesses. Although these events are unfortunate, none of them involve Bitcoin itself being hacked, nor imply inherent flaws in Bitcoin; just like a bank robbery doesn't mean that the dollar is compromised. However, it is accurate to say that a complete set of good practices and intuitive security solutions is needed to give users better protection of their money, and to reduce the general risk of theft and loss. Over the course of the last few years, such security features have quickly developed, such as wallet encryption, offline wallets, hardware wallets, and multi-signature transactions.

9.1.44   COULD USERS COLLUDE AGAINST BITCOIN?

It is not possible to change the Bitcoin protocol that easily. Any Bitcoin client that doesn't comply with the same rules cannot enforce their own rules on other users. As per the current specification, double spending is not possible on the same block chain, and neither is spending bitcoins without a valid signature. Therefore, It is not possible to generate uncontrolled amounts of bitcoins out of thin air, spend other users' funds, corrupt the network, or anything similar.

However, powerful miners could arbitrarily choose to block or reverse recent transactions. A majority of users can also put pressure for some changes to be adopted. Because Bitcoin only works correctly with a complete consensus between all users, changing the protocol can be very difficult and requires an overwhelming majority of users to adopt the changes in such a way that remaining users have nearly no choice but to follow. As a general rule, it is hard to imagine why any

Bitcoin user would choose to adopt any change that could compromise their own money.

9.1.45   IS BITCOIN VULNERABLE TO QUANTUM COMPUTING?

Yes, most systems relying on cryptography in general are, including traditional banking systems. However, quantum computers don't yet exist and probably won't for a while. In the event that quantum computing could be an imminent threat to Bitcoin, the protocol could be upgraded to use post-quantum algorithms. Given the importance that this update would have, it can be safely expected that it would be highly reviewed by developers and adopted by all Bitcoin users.

10 CRYPTOGRAPHY USED IN BITCOIN

All currencies need some way to control supply and enforce various security properties to prevent cheating. In fiat currencies, organizations like central banks control the money supply and add anti-counterfeiting features to physical currency. These security features raise the bar for an attacker, but they don't make money impossible to counterfeit. Ultimately, law enforcement is necessary for stopping people from breaking the rules of the system.

Cryptocurrencies too must have security measures that prevent people from tampering with the state of the system, and from equivocating, that is, making mutually inconsistent statements to different people. If Alice convinces Bob that she paid him a digital coin, for example, she should not be able to convince Carol that she paid her that same coin. But unlike fiat currencies, the security rules of cryptocurrencies need to be enforced purely technologically and without relying on a central authority.

As the word suggests, cryptocurrencies make heavy use of cryptography. Cryptography provides a mechanism for securely encoding the rules of a cryptocurrency system in the system itself. We can use it to prevent tampering and equivocation, as well as to encode the rules for creation of new units of the currency into a mathematical protocol. Before we can properly understand cryptocurrencies then, we'll need to delve into the cryptographic foundations that they rely upon.

Cryptography is a deep academic research field utilizing many advanced mathematical techniques that are notoriously subtle and complicated to understand. Fortunately, Bitcoin only relies on a handful of relatively simple and well-known cryptographic constructions. In this chapter, we'll specifically study cryptographic hashes and digital signatures, two primitives that prove to be very useful for building cryptocurrencies. Future chapters will introduce more complicated cryptographic schemes, such as zero-knowledge proofs, that are used in proposed extensions and modifications to

Bitcoin.

Once we've learnt the necessary cryptographic primitives, we'll discuss some of the ways in which those are used to build cryptocurrencies. We'll complete this chapter with some examples of simple cryptocurrencies that illustrate some of the design challenges that we need to deal with.

10.1 Cryptographic Hash Functions

The first cryptographic primitive that we'll need to understand is a *cryptographic hash function.* A

hash function is a mathematical function with the following three properties:

- Its input can be any string of any size.

- It produces a fixed size output. For the purpose of making the discussion in this chapter concrete, we will assume a 256-bit output size. However, our discussion holds true for any output size as long as it is sufficiently large.

- It is efficiently computable. Intuitively this means that for a given input string, you can figure

out what the output of the hash function is in a reasonable amount of time. More technically, computing the hash of an n - bit string should have a running time that is $O(n)$.

Those properties define a general hash function, one that could be used to build a data structure such as a hash table. We're going to focus exclusively on c *ryptographic* hash functions. For a hash function to be cryptographically secure, we're going to require that it has the following three additional properties: (1) collision-resistance,

(2) hiding, (3) puzzle-friendliness.

We'll look more closely at each of these properties to gain an understanding of why it's useful to have a function that behaves that way. The reader who has studied cryptography should be aware that the treatment of hash functions in this book is a bit different from a standard cryptography textbook. The puzzle-friendliness property, in particular, is not a general requirement for cryptographic hash functions, but one that will be useful for cryptocurrencies specifically.

Property 1: Collision-resistance. The first property that we need from a cryptographic hash function is that it's collision-resistant. A collision occurs when two distinct inputs produce the same output. A hash function $H(.)$ is collision-resistant if nobody can find a collision. Formally:

Figure 1.1 A hash collision. x a nd y are distinct values, yet when input into hash function H , they produce the same output.

Notice that we said *n obody can find* a collision, but we did not say that no collisions exist. Actually, we know for a fact that collisions do exist, and we can prove this by a simple counting argument. The input space to the hash function contains all strings of all lengths, yet the output space contains only strings of a specific fixed length. Because the input space is larger than the output space (indeed, the input space is infinite, while the output space is finite), there must be input strings that map to the same output string. In fact, by the Pigeonhole Principle there will necessarily be a very large number of possible inputs that map to any particular output.

Collision-resistance: A hash function H is said to be collision resistant if it is infeasible to find t wo values, x and y , such that $x =/y$, yet $H(x) = H(y)$.

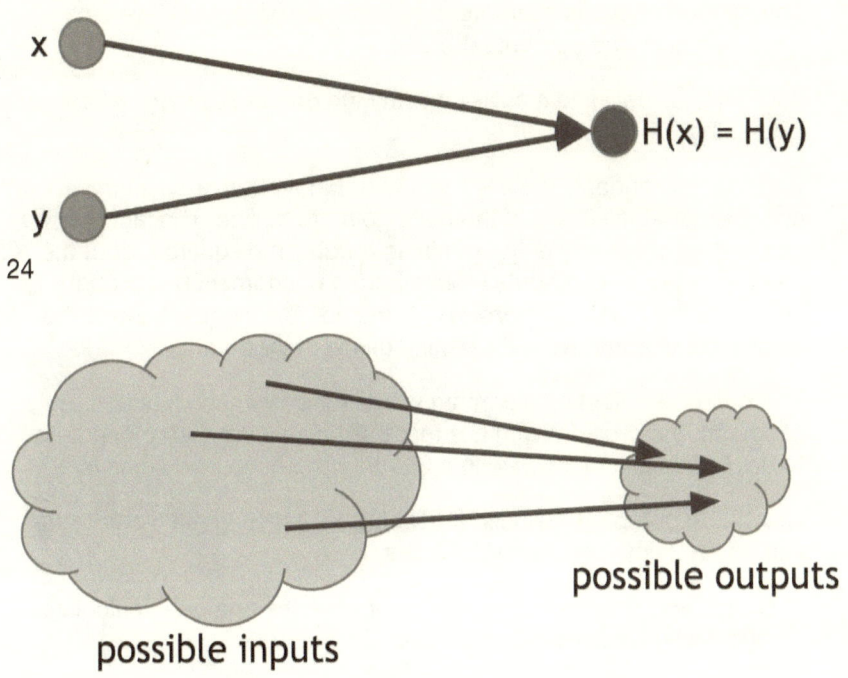

x

y

24

H(x) = H(y)

possible outputs

possible inputs

Figure 1.2 B e c a u s e t h e n u m b e r o f i n p u t s e x c e e d s
t h e n u m b e r o f o u t p u t s , w e a r e g u a r a n t e e d t h a t
there must be at least one output to which the hash function maps
more than one input.

Now, to make things even worse, we said that it has to be impossible
to find a collision. Yet, there are methods that are guaranteed to find a
collision. Consider the following simple method for finding a

256 collision for a hash function with a 256-bit output size: pick 2 + 1
distinct values, compute the

hashes of each of them, and check if there are any two outputs are
equal. Since we picked more inputs than possible outputs, some pair
of them must collide when you apply the hash function.

The method above is guaranteed to find a collision. But if we pick random inputs and compute the 256

hash values, we'll find a collision with high probability long before examining 2 + 1 inputs. In fact, if 130

we randomly choose just 2 + 1 inputs, it turns out there's a 99.8% chance that at least two of them are going to collide. The fact that we can find a collision by only examining roughly the square root of the number of possible outputs results from a phenomenon in probability known as the *b irthday paradox*. In the homework questions at the end of this chapter, we will examine this in more detail.

This collision-detection algorithm works for every hash function. But, of course, the problem with it is that this takes a very, very long time to do. For a hash function with a 256-bit output, you would have

256 128 to compute the hash function 2 + 1 times in the worst case, and about 2 times on average. That's

of course an astronomically large number — if a computer calculates 10,000 hashes per second, it 27 128

would take more than one octillion (10) years to calculate 2 hashes! For another way of thinking about this, we can say that, if every computer ever made by humanity was computing since the beginning of the entire universe, up to now, the odds that they would have found a collision is still infinitesimally small. So small that it's way less than the odds that the Earth will be destroyed by a giant meteor in the next two seconds.

We have thus seen a general but impractical algorithm to find a collision for *a ny* h ash function. A more difficult question is: is there some other method that could be used on a particular hash function in order to find a collision? In other words, although the generic collision detection algorithm is not feasible to use, there still may be some other algorithm that can efficiently find a collision for a specific hash function.

Consider, for example, the following hash function:

$$H(x) = x \bmod 2^{256}$$

This function meets our requirements of a hash function as it accepts inputs of any length, returns a

fixed sized output (256 bits), and is efficiently computable. But this function also has an efficient

method for finding a collision. Notice that this function just returns the last 256 bits of the input. One 256

collision then would be the values 3 and 3 + 2 . This simple example illustrates that even though our generic collision detection method is not usable in practice, there are at least some hash functions for which an efficient collision detection method does exist.

Yet for other hash functions, we don't know if such methods exist. We suspect that they are collision resistant. However, there are no hash functions *p roven* to be collision-resistant. The cryptographic hash functions that we rely on in practice are just functions for which people have tried really, really hard to find collisions and haven't yet succeeded. In some cases, such as the old MD5 hash function, collisions were eventually found after years of work, leading the function to be deprecated and phased out of practical use. And so we choose to believe that those are collision resistant.

Application: Message digests N ow that we know what collision-resistance is, the logical question is: What is collision-resistance useful for? Here's one application: If we know that two inputs x and y to a collision-resistant hash function H a re different, then it's safe to assume that their hashes $H(x)$ and $H(y)$ a r e d i f f e r e n t — i f s o m e o n e k n e w a n x a n d y t h a t w e r e d i f f e r e n t b u t h a d t h e s a m e h a s h , t h a t would violate our assumption that H is collision resistant.

This argument allows us to use hash outputs as a ***m essage digest***. Consider SecureBox, an authenticated online file storage system that allows users to upload files and ensure their integrity when they download them. Suppose that Alice uploads really large file, and wants to be able to verify later that the file she downloads is the same as the one she uploads. One way to do that would be to save the whole big file locally, and directly compare it to the file she downloads. While this works, it largely defeats the purpose of uploading it in the first place; if Alice needs to have access to a local copy of the file to ensure its integrity, she can just use the local copy directly.

Collision-free hashes provide an elegant and efficient solution to this problem. Alice just needs to remember the hash of the original file. When she later downloads the file from SecureBox, she computes the hash of the downloaded file and compares it to the one she stored. If the hashes are the same, then she can conclude that the file is indeed the one she uploaded, but if they are different, then Alice can conclude that the file has been tampered with. Remembering the hash thus allows her to detect *a ccidental* corruption of the file during transmission or on SecureBox's servers, but also *intentional* modification of the file by the server. Such guarantees in the face of potentially malicious behavior by other entities are at the core of what cryptography gives us.

The hash serves as a fixed length digest, or unambiguous summary, of a message. This gives us a very efficient way to remember things we've seen before and recognize them again. Whereas the entire file might have been gigabytes long, the hash is of fixed length, 256-bits for the hash function in our example. This greatly reduces our storage requirement. Later in this chapter and throughout the book, we'll see applications for which it's useful to use a hash as a message digest.

Property 2: Hiding T he second property that we want from our hash functions is that it's **hiding**. The hiding property asserts that if we're given the output of the hash function $y = H(x)$, there's no feasible way to figure out what the input, x, was. The problem is that this property can't be true in the stated form. Consider the following simple example: we're going to do an experiment where we flip a coin. If the result of the coin flip was heads, we're going to announce the hash of the string "heads". If the result was tails, we're going to announce the hash of the string "tails".

We then ask someone, an adversary, who didn't see the coin flip, but only saw this hash output, to figure out what the string was that was hashed (we'll soon see why we might want to play games like this). In response, they would simply compute both the hash of the string "heads" and the hash of the string "tails", and they could see which one they were given. And so, in just a couple steps, they can figure out what the input was.

The adversary was able to guess what the string was because there were only two possible values of x, and it was easy for the adversary to just try both of them. In order to be able to achieve the hiding property, it needs to be the case that there's no value of x which is particularly likely. That is, x has to be chosen from a set that's, in some sense, very spread out. If x is chosen from such a set, this method of trying a few values of x that are especially likely will not work.

The big question is: can we achieve the hiding property when the values that we want do not come from a spread-out set as in our "heads" and "tails" experiment? Fortunately, the answer is yes! So pe rhaps we can h i d e e v e n a n i n p u t t h a t ' s n o t s p r e a d o u t b y c o n c a t e n a t i n g i t w i t h a n o t h e r i n p u t t h a t *i* s spread out. We can now be slightly more precise about what we mean by hiding (the double vertical bar ‖ denotes concatenation).

In information-theory, ***m in-entropy*** i s a measure of how predictable an outcome is, and high

min-entropy captures the intuitive idea that the distribution (i.e., random variable) is very spread out.

What that means specifically is that when we sample from the distribution, there's no particular value

Hiding. A hash function H is hiding if: when a secret value r is chosen from a probability distribution that has *h igh min-entropy*, then given H $(r ‖ x)$ it is infeasible to find x .

that's likely to occur. So, for a concrete example, if r is chosen uniformly from among all of the strings 256 that are 256 bits long, then any particular string was chosen with probability $1/2$, which is an infinitesimally small value.

Application: Commitments. N ow let's look at an application of the hiding property. In particular, what we want to do is something called a **c ommitment**. A commitment is the digital analog of taking a value, sealing it in an envelope, and putting that envelope out on the table where everyone can see it. When you do that, you've committed yourself to what's inside the envelope. But you haven't opened it, so even though you've committed to a value, the value remains a secret from everyone else. Later, you can open the envelope and reveal the value that you committed to earlier.

Commitment scheme. A commitment scheme consists of two algorithms:

- **com := commit(m sg, nonce)** T he commit function takes a message and secret random value, called a nonce, as input and returns a commitment.

- **verify(c om, msg, nonce)** T he verify function takes a commitment, nonce, and message as input. It returns true if $com ==$ commit(m sg, n once) and false otherwise. We require that the following two security properties hold:

- *Hiding*: Given c om, it is infeasible to find m sg

- *Binding*: It is infeasible to find two pairs (msg, nonce) and (msg', nonce') such that m sg $\neq msg'$ and commit(m sg, nonce) $==$ commit(m sg', nonce')

To use a commitment scheme, we first need to generate a random *n once*. W e then apply the *c ommit* function to this nonce together with *m sg*, the value being committed to, and we publish the commitment *c om*. This stage is analogous to putting the sealed envelope on the table. At a later point, if we want to reveal the value that they committed to earlier, we publish the random nonce that we used to create this commitment, and the message, *msg*. Now, anybody can verify that *m sg* was indeed the message committed to earlier. This stage is analogous to opening up the envelope.

The two security properties dictate that the algorithms actually behave like sealing and opening an envelope. First, given *c om*, the commitment, someone looking at the envelope can't figure out what the message is. The second property is that it's binding. This ensures that when you commit to what's in the envelope, you can't change your mind later. That is, it's infeasible to find two different messages, such that you can commit to one message, and then later claim that you committed to another.

So how do we know that these two properties hold? Before we can answer this, we need to discuss how we're going to actually implement a commitment scheme. We can do so using a cryptographic hash function. Consider the following commitment scheme:

commit(*m sg, nonce*) := H(*n once* ‖ *msg*) where *n once* is a random 256-bit value

To commit to a message, we generate a random 256-bit nonce. Then we concatenate the nonce and the message and return the hash of this concatenated value as the commitment. To verify, someone will compute this same hash of the nonce they were given concatenated with the message. And they will check whether that's equal to the commitment that they saw.

Take another look at the two properties that we require of our commitment schemes. If we substitute the instantiation of *c ommit* a nd *v erify* a s well as *H (nonce* ‖ *msg)* f or *c om*, then these properties

Everytime you commit to a value , i t i s i m p o r t a n t t h a t y o u c h o o s e a n e w r a n d o m v a l u e *n o n c e* . I n cryptography, the term *n once* is used to refer to a value that can only be used once.

become:

- *Hiding*: Given H(*n once* ‖ *msg*), it is infeasible to find *m sg*

- *Binding*: It is infeasible to find two pairs *(msg, nonce)* and (

msg', nonce') such that *m sg* $\neq$ */msg'* and H(*n once* ∥ *msg*) == H(*n once'* ∥ *msg'*) The *h iding* p roperty of commitments is exactly the hiding property that we required for our hash functions . If *key* was chosen as a random 2 5 6 - b i t v a l u e t h e n t h e h i d i n g p r o p e r t y s a y s t h a t i f w e h a s h t h e c o n c a t e n a t i o n o f *k e y* a n d t h e m e s s a g e , t h e n i t ' s i n f e a s i b l e t o r e c o v e r t h e m e s s a g e f r o m t h e h a s h output. And it turns out that the *b inding property* i s

implied by[1] the collision-resistant property of the underlying hash function. If the hash function is collision-resistant, then it will be infeasible to find distinct values msg and msg' such that H(*n once* ∥ *msg*) = H (*n once'* ∥ *msg'*) since such values would indeed be a collision. Therefore, if *H* is a hash function that is collision-resistant and hiding, this commitment scheme will work, in the sense that it will have the necessary security properties.

Property 3: Puzzle friendliness. The third security property we're going to need from hash functions is that they are puzzle-friendly. This property is a bit complicated. We will first explain what the technical requirements of this property are and then give an application that illustrates why this property is useful. Intuitively, what this means is that if someone wants to target the hash function to come out to some particular output value *y* , that if there's part of the input that is chosen in a suitably randomized way, it's very difficult to find another value that hits exactly that target. ***Application: Search puzzle.*** Now, let's consider an application that illustrates the usefulness of this property. In this application, we're going to build a ***s earch puzzle***, a mathematical problem which requires searching a very large space in order to find the solution. In particular, a search puzzle has no shortcuts. That is, there's no way to find a valid solution other than searching that large space. [1] The reverse implications do not hold. That is, it's possible that you can find collisions, but none of them are of the form H(*n once*∥*msg*)==H (*n once'*∥*msg'*). Forexample, if you can only findacollision in which two distinct nonces generate the same commitment for the same message, then the commitment scheme is still binding, but the underlying hash function is not collision-resistant.

Puzzle friendliness. A hash function H is said to be puzzle-friendly if for every possible n-bit output value y, if k is chosen from a distribution with high min-entropy, then it is infeasible to find x such n that H(k ‖ x) = y in time significantly less than 2.

Search puzzle. A search puzzle consists of

- a hash function, H,

- a value, id (which we call the **puzzle-ID**), chosen from a high min-entropy distribution

- and a target set Y A solution to this puzzle is a value, x, such that H $(id ‖ x)$ ∈ Y.

n The intuition is this: if H has an n-bit output, then it can take any of 2 values. Solving the puzzle

requires finding an input so that the output falls within the set Y, which is typically much smaller than the set of all outputs. The size of Y determines how hard the puzzle is. If Y is the set of all n-bit strings the puzzle is trivial, whereas if Y has only 1 element the puzzle is maximally hard. The fact that the puzzle id has high min-entropy ensures that there are no shortcuts. On the contrary, if a particular value of the ID were likely, then someone could cheat, say by pre-computing a solution to the puzzle with that ID.

If a search puzzle is puzzle-friendly, this implies that there's no solving strategy for this puzzle which is much better than just trying random values of x. And so, if we want to pose a puzzle that's difficult to solve, we can do it this way as long as we can generate puzzle-IDs in a suitably random way. We're going to use this idea later when we talk about Bitcoin mining, which is a sort of computational puzzle.

SHA-256. We've discussed three properties of hash functions, and one application of each of those. Now let's discuss a particular hash function that we're going to use a lot in this book. There are lots of hash functions in existence, but this is the one Bitcoin uses primarily, and it's a pretty good one to use. It's called *S H A - 2 5 6*.

Recall that we require that our hash functions work on inputs of arbitrary length. Luckily, as long aswe can build a hash function that works on fixed-length inputs, there's a generic method to convert it into a hash function that works on arbitrary-length inputs. It's called the *M erkle-Damgard transform*. SHA-256 is one of a number of commonly used hash functions that make use of this method. In common terminology, the underlying fixed-length collision-resistant hash function is called the *compression function*. It has been proven that if the underlying compression function is collision resistant, then the overall hash function is collision resistant as well.

The Merkle-Damgard transform is quite simple. Say the compression function takes inputs of length m and produces an output of a smaller length n. The input to the hash function, which can be of any size, is divided into *blocks* of length $m - n$. The construction works as follows: pass each block together with the output of the previous block into the compression function. Notice that input length will then be $(m - n) + n = m$, which is the input length to the compression function. For the first block, to which

there is no previous block output, we instead use an *Initialization Vector (IV)*. This number is reused for every call to the hash function, and in practice you can just look it up in a standards document. The last block's output is the result that you return.

SHA-256 uses a compression function that takes 768-bit input and produces 256-bit outputs. The block size is 512 bits. See Figure 1.3 for a graphical depiction of how SHA-256 works.

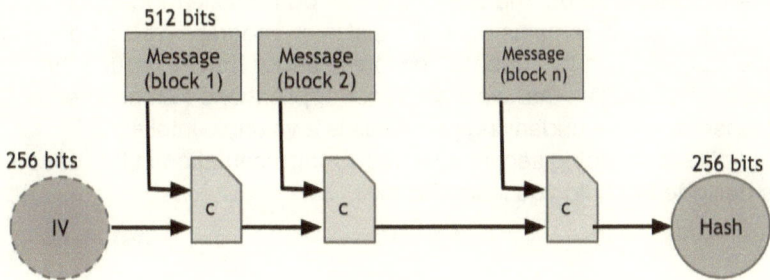

*Figure 1.3: SHA-256 Hash Function (simplified
). SHA-256 uses the Merkle-Damgard transform t
o turn* a fixed-length collision-resistant compression function into a
hash function that accepts arbitrary-length inputs. The input is
"padded" so that its length is a multiple of 512 bits.

We've talked about hash functions, cryptographic hash functions with
special properties, applications of those properties, and a specific
hash function that we use in Bitcoin. In the next section, we'll discuss
ways of using hash functions to build more complicated data
structures that are used in distributed systems like Bitcoin.

Sidebar: modeling hash functions. Hash functions are the Swiss
Army knife of cryptography: they find a place in a spectacular variety
of applications. The flip side to this versatility is that different
applications require slightly different properties of hash functions to
ensure security. It's proven notoriously hard to pin down a list of hash
function properties that would result in provable security across the
board.

In this text, we've selected three properties that are crucial to the way
that hash functions are used in Bitcoin and other cryptocurrencies.
Even within this space, not all of these properties are necessary for
every use of hash functions. For example, puzzle-friendliness is only
important in Bitcoin mining, as we'll see.

Designers of secure systems often throw in the towel and model hash
functions as functions that output an independent random value for

every possible input. The use of this "random oracle model" for proving security remains controversial in cryptography. Regardless of one's position on this debate, reasoning about how to reduce the security properties that we want in our applications to fundamental properties of the underlying primitives is a valuable intellectual exercise for building secure systems. Our presentation in this chapter is designed to help you learn this skill.

1.2 Hash Pointers and Data Structures

In this section , we are going t o d i s c u s s *h a s h p o i n t e r s* a n
d t h e i r a p p l i c a t i o n s . A h a s h p o i n t e r i s a d a t a
structure that turns out to be useful in many of the systems that we will talk about. A hash pointer is simply a pointer to where some information is stored together with a cryptographic hash of the information. Whereas a regular pointer gives you a way to retrieve the information, a hash pointer also gives you a way to verify that the information hasn't changed.

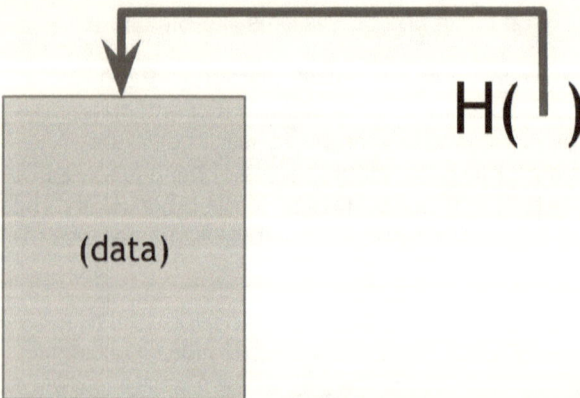

Figure 1.4 Hash pointer. A hash pointer is a pointer to where data is stored together with a cryptographic hash of the value of that data at some fixed point in time.

We can use hash pointers to build all kinds of data structures. Intuitively, we can take a familiar data structure that uses pointers such as a linked list or a binary search tree and implement it with hash pointers, instead of pointers as we normally would.

Block chain. I n Figure 1.5, we built a linked list using hash pointers. We're going to call this data structure a **b lock chain**. Whereas as in a regular linked list where you have a series of blocks, each block has data as well as a pointer to the previous block in the list, in a block chain the previous block pointer will be replaced with a hash pointer. So each block not only tells us where the value of the previous block was, but it also contains a digest of that value that allows us to verify that the value hasn't changed. We store the head of the list, which is just a regular hash-pointer that points to the most recent data block.

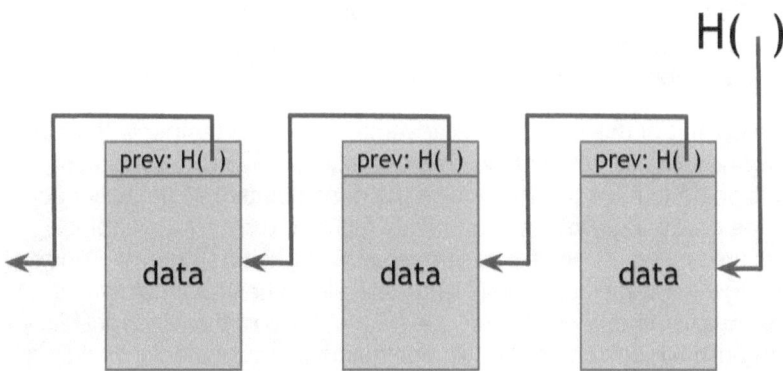

Figure 1.5 Block chain. A block chain is a linked list that is built with hash pointers instead of pointers.

A use case for a block chain is a **tamper-evident log**. That is, we want to build a log data structure that stores a bunch of data, and allows us to append data onto the end of the log. But If somebody alters data that is earlier in the log, we're going to detect it.

To understand why a block chain achieves this tamper-evident property, let's ask what happens if an adversary wants to tamper with data that's in the middle of the chain. Specifically, the adversary's goal is to do it in such a way that someone who remembers only the hash pointer at the head of the block chain won't be able to detect the tampering. To achieve this goal, the adversary changes the data of some block k. Since the data has been changed, the hash in block $k+1$, which is a hash of the entire block k, is not going to match up. Remember that we are statistically guaranteed that the new hash will not match the altered content since the hash function is collision resistant. And so we will detect the inconsistency between the new data in block k and the hash pointer in block $k+1$.

Of course the adversary can continue to try and cover up this change by changing the next block's hash as well. The adversary can continue doing this, but this strategy will fail when he reaches the head of the list. Specifically, as long as we store the hash pointer at the head of the list in a place where the adversary cannot change it, the adversary will be unable to change any block without being detected.

The upshot of this is that if the adversary wants to tamper with data anywhere in this entire chain, in order to keep the story consistent, he's going to have to tamper with the hash pointers all the way back to the beginning. And he's ultimately going to run into a roadblock because he won't be able to tamper with the head of the list. Thus it emerges, that by just remembering this single hash pointer, we've essentially remembered a tamper-evident hash of the entire list. So we can build a block chain like this containing as many blocks as we want, going back to some special block at the beginning of the list, which we will call the **genesis block**.

You may have noticed that the block chain construction is similar to the Merkle-Damgard construction that we saw in the previous section. Indeed, they are quite similar, and the same security argument applies to both of them.

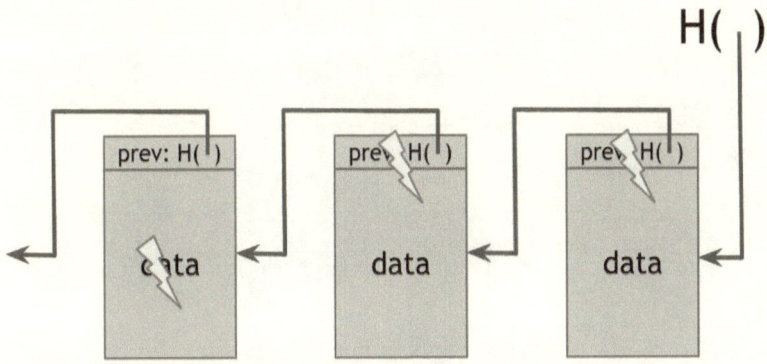

Figure 1.6 Tamper-evident log. If an adversary modifies data anywhere in the block chain, it will result in the hash pointer in the following block being incorrect. If we store the head of the list, then even if the adversary modifies all of the pointers to be consistent with the modified data, the head pointer will be incorrect, and we will detect the tampering.

Merkle trees. A nother useful data structure that we can build using hash pointers is a binary tree. A binary tree with hash pointers is known as a ***M erkle tree***, after its inventor Ralph Merkle. Suppose we have a number of blocks containing data. These blocks comprise the leaves of our tree. We group these data blocks into pairs of two, and then for each pair, we build a data structure that has two hash pointers, one to each of these blocks. These data structures make the next level up of the tree. We in turn group these into groups of two, and for each pair, create a new data structure that contains the hash of each. We continue doing this until we reach a single block, the root of the tree.

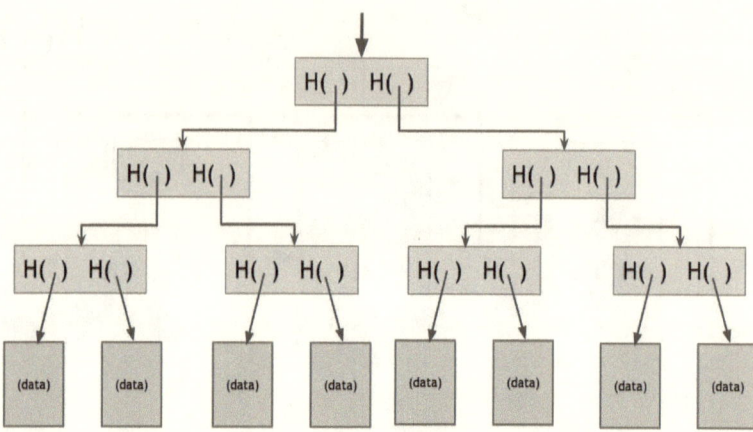

Figure 1.7 Merkle tree. I n a Merkle tree, data blocks are grouped in pairs and the hash of each of these blocks is stored in a parent node. The parent nodes are in turn grouped in pairs and their hashes stored one level up the tree. This continues all the way up the tree until we reach the root node.

As before, we remember just the hash pointer at the head of the tree. We now have the ability traverse down through the hash pointers to any point in the list. This allows us make sure that the data hasn't been tampered with because, just like we saw with the block chain, if an adversary tampers with some data block at the bottom of the tree, that will cause the hash pointer that's one level up to not match, and even if he continues to tamper with this block, the change will eventually propagate to the top of the tree where he won't be able to tamper with the hash pointer that we've stored. So again, any attempt to tamper with any piece of data will be detected by just remembering the hash pointer at the top.

Proof of membership. A nother nice feature of Merkle trees is that, unlike the block chain that we built before, it allows a concise proof of membership. Say that someone wants to prove that a certain data block is a member of the Merkle Tree. As usual, we remember just the root. Then they need to show us this data block, and the blocks on the path from the data block to the root. We can ignore the rest of the tree, as the blocks on this path are enough to allow us to verify the hashes all the way up to the root of the tree. See Figure 1.8 for a graphical depiction of how this works.

If there are *n* nodes in the tree, only about *log(n)* items need to be shown. And since each step just r e q u i r e s c o m p u t i n g t h e h a s h of the child block , i t t a k e s a b o u t *l o g (n)* t i m e f o r u s t o v e r i f y i t . A n d s o even if the Merkle tree contains a very large number of blocks, we can still prove membership in a relatively short time. Verification thus runs in time and space that's logarithmic in the number of nodes in the tree.

F i g u r e 1 . 8 Proof of membership . To prove t h a t a d a t a b l o c k i s i n c l u d e d i n t h e t r e e , o n e o n l y n e e d s t o show the blocks in the path from that data block to the root.

A *sorted Merkle tree* is just a Merkle tree where we take the blocks at the bottom, and we sort them using some ordering function. This can be alphabetical, lexicographical order, numerical order, or some other agreed upon ordering.

Proof of non-membership. W ith a sorted Merkle tree, it becomes possible to verify non-membership in a logarithmic time and space. That is, we can prove that a particular block is not in the Merkle tree. And the way we do that is simply by showing a path to the item that's just before where the item in question would be and showing the path to the item that is just after where it would be. If these two items are consecutive in the tree, then this serves as a proof that the item in question is not included. For if it was included, it would need to be between the two items shown, but there is no space between them as they are consecutive.

We've discussed using hash pointers in linked lists and binary trees, but more generally, it turns out that we can use hash pointers in any pointer-based data structure as long as the data structure doesn't have cycles. If there are cycles in the data structure, then we won't be able to make all the hashes match up. If you think about it, in an acyclic data structure, we can start near the leaves, or near the things that don't have any pointers coming out of them, compute the hashes of those, and then work our way back toward the beginning. But in a structure with cycles, there's no end we can start with and compute back from.

So, to consider another example, we can build a directed acyclic graph out of hash pointers. And we'll be able to verify membership in that graph very efficiently. And it will be easy to compute. Using hash pointers in this way is a general trick that you'll see time and again in the context of the distributed data structures and throughout the algorithms that we discuss later in this chapter.

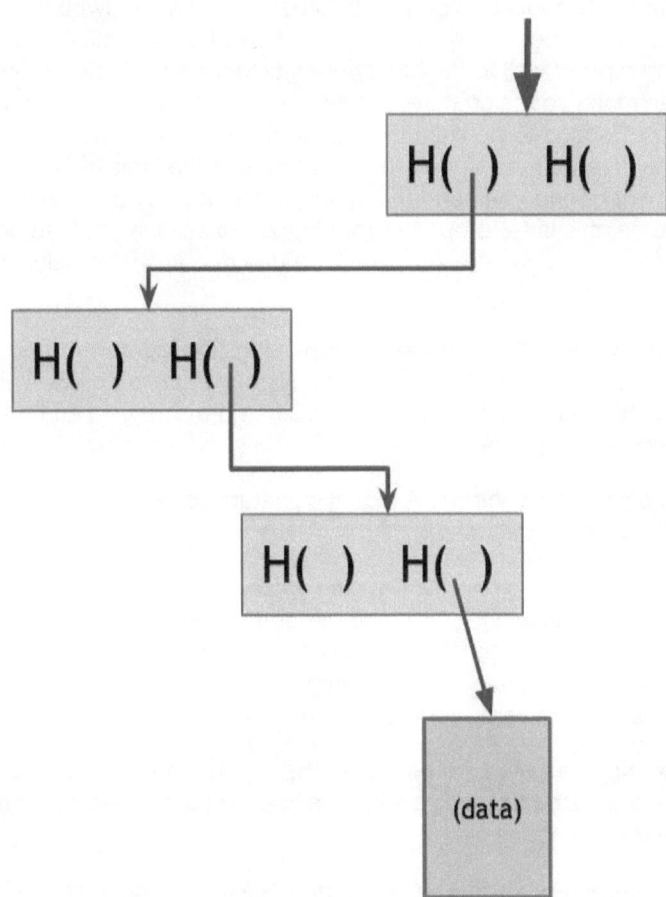

10.2 Digital Signatures

In this section, we'll look at **digital signatures**. This is the second cryptographic primitive, along with hash functions, that we need as building blocks for the cryptocurrency discussion later on. A digital signature is supposed to be the digital analog to a handwritten signature on paper. We desire two properties from digital signatures that correspond well to the handwritten signature analogy. Firstly, only you can make your signature, but anyone who sees it can verify that it's valid. Secondly, we want the signature to be tied to a particular document so that the signature cannot be used to indicate your agreement or endorsement of a different document. For handwritten signatures, this latter property is analogous to assuring that somebody can't take your signature and snip it off one document and glue it onto the bottom of another one.

How can we build this in a digital form using cryptography? First, let's make the previous intuitive discussion slightly more concrete. This will allow us to reason better about digital signature schemes and discuss their security properties.

Digital signature scheme. A digital signature scheme consists of the following three algorithms:

- **(sk, pk) := generateKeys(*k eysize*)** T he generateKeys method takes a key size and generates a key pair. The secret key *s k* is kept privately and used to sign messages. *p k* i s the public verification key that you give to everybody. Anyone with this key can verify your signature.

- **sig := sign(*s k, m essage*)** T he sign method takes a message and a secret key, *s k*, a s input and outputs a signature for *m essage* u nder *s k*

- **isValid := verify(*p k, m essage, s ig*)** T he verify method takes a message, a signature, and a public key as input. It returns a boolean value, *i sValid*, that will be **t *rue*** if *s ig* is a valid signature for *m essage* under public key *p k*, and **f *alse*** o therwise. We require that the following two properties hold:

- *Valid signatures must verify* **verify**(*p k, m essage,* **s ign**(*s k, m essage*)) == **t rue**

- Signatures are **e *xistentially unforgeable***

We note that **generateKeys** and **sign** can be randomized algorithms. Indeed, generateKeys had better be randomized because it ought to be generating different keys for different people. **v erify**, on the other hand, will always be deterministic.

Let us now examine the two properties that we require of a digital signature scheme in more detail. The first property is straightforward — that valid signatures must verify. If I sign a message with $s\ k$, my secret key, and someone later tries to validate that signature over that same message using my public key, $p\ k$, the signature must validate correctly. This property is a basic requirement for signatures to be useful at all.

Unforgeability. T he second requirement is that it's computationally infeasible to forge signatures. That is, an adversary who knows your public key and gets to see your signatures on some other messages can't forge your signature on some message for which he has not seen your signature. This unforgeability property is generally formalized in terms of a game that we play with an adversary. The use of games is quite common in cryptographic security proofs.

In the unforgeability game, there is an adversary who claims that he can forge signatures and a challenger that will test this claim. The first thing we do is we use **generateKeys** to generate a secret signing key and a corresponding public verification key. We give the secret key to the challenger, and we give the public key to both the challenger and to the adversary. So the adversary only knows information that's public, and his mission is to try to forge a message. The challenger knows the secret key. So he can make signatures.

Intuitively, the setup of this game matches real world conditions. A real-life attacker would likely be able to see valid signatures from their would-be victim on a number of different documents. And maybe the attacker could even manipulate the victim into signing innocuous-looking documents if that's useful to the attacker.

To model this in our game, we're going to allow the attacker to get signatures on some documents of his choice, for as long as he wants, as long as the number of guesses is plausible. To give an intuitive

idea of what we mean by a plausible number of guesses, we would allow the attacker to try 1 million 80 2

guesses, but not 2 guesses .

Once the attacker is satisfied that he's seen enough signatures, then the attacker picks some message, M, that they will attempt to forge a signature on. The only restriction on M is that it must be a message for which the attacker has not previously seen a signature (because the attacker can obviously send back a signature that he was given).

The challenger runs the **v erify** algorithm to determine if the signature produced by the attacker is a valid signature on M under the public verification key. If it successfully verifies, the attacker wins the game.

---

2 In asymptotic terms, we allow the attacker to try a number of guesses that is a polynomial function of the key size, but no more (e.g. the attacker cannot try exponentially many guesses).

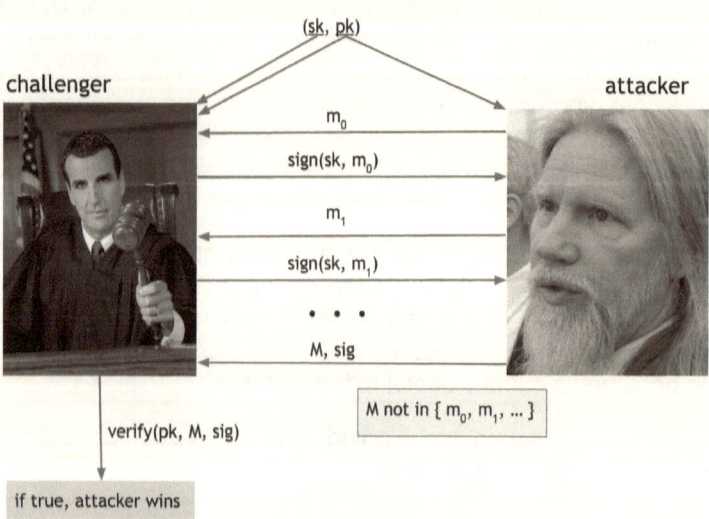

Figure 1.9 Unforgeability game. T he adversary and the challenger play the unforgeability game. If the attacker is able to successfully output a signature on a message that he has not previously seen, he wins. If he is unable, the challenger wins and the digital signature scheme is unforgeable.

We say that the signature scheme is unforgeable if and only if, no matter what algorithm the adversary is using, his chance of successfully forging a message is extremely small — so small that we can assume it will never happen in practice.

Practical Concerns. T here are a number of practical things that we need to do to turn the algorithmic idea into a digital signature mechanism that can be implemented in practice. For example, many signature algorithms are randomized (in particular the one used in Bitcoin) and we therefore need a good source of randomness. The importance of this really can't be underestimated as bad randomness will make your otherwise-secure algorithm insecure.

Another practical concern is the message size. In practice, there's a limit on the message size that you're able to sign because real schemes are going to operate on bit strings of limited length. There's an easy way around this limitation: sign the hash of the message, rather than the message itself. If we use a cryptographic hash function with a 256-bit output, then we can effectively sign a message of any length as long as our signature scheme can sign 256-bit messages. As we discussed before, it's safe to use the hash of the message as a message digest in this manner since the hash function is collision resistant.

Another trick that we will use later is that you can sign a hash pointer. If you sign a hash pointer, then the signature covers, or protects, the whole structure — not just the hash pointer itself, but everything the chain of hash pointers points to. For example, if you were to sign the hash pointer that was at the end of a block chain, the result is that you would effectively be digitally signing the that entire block chain.

ECDSA. N ow let's get into the nuts and bolts. Bitcoin uses a particular digital signature scheme that's called the Elliptic Curve Digital Signature Algorithm (ECDSA). ECDSA is a U.S. government standard, an update of the earlier DSA algorithm adapted to use elliptic curves. These algorithms have received considerable cryptographic analysis over the years and are generally believed to be secure.

More specifically, Bitcoin uses ECDSA over the standard elliptic curve "secp256k1" which is estimated 128

to provide 128 bits of security (that is, it is as difficult to break this algorithm as performing 2 symmetric-key cryptographic operations such as invoking a hash function). While this curve is a published standard, it is rarely used outside of Bitcoin, with other applications using ECDSA (such as key exchange in TLS for secure web browsing) typically using the more common "secp256r1" curve. This is just a quirk of Bitcoin, as this was chosen by Satoshi in the early specification of the system and is now difficult to change.

We won't go into all the details of how ECDSA works as there's some complicated math involved, and understanding it is not necessary for any other content in this book. I f you're interested in the details, refer to our further reading section at the end of this chapter. It might be useful to have an idea of the sizes of various quantities, however:

Private key: Public key, uncompressed: Public key, compressed: Message to be signed: Signature:

256 bits 512 bits 257 bits 256 bits 512 bits

Note that while ECDSA can technically only sign messages 256 bits long, this is not a problem: messages are always hashed before being signed, so effectively any size message can be efficiently signed.

With ECDSA, a good source of randomness is essential because a bad source of randomness will likely leak your key. It makes intuitive sense that if you use bad randomness in generating a key, then the key you generate will likely not be secure. But it's a quirk of ECDSA[3] that, even if you use bad

randomness just in making a signature, using your perfectly good key, that also will leak your private key. And then it's game over; if you leak your private key, an adversary can forge your signature. We thus need to be especially careful about using good randomness in practice, and using a bad source of randomness is a common pitfall of otherwise secure systems.

This completes our discussion of digital signatures as a cryptographic primitive. In the next section, we'll discuss some applications of digital signatures that will turn out to be useful for building cryptocurrencies.

Sidebar: cryptocurrencies and encryption. If you've been waiting to find out which encryption algorithm is used in Bitcoin, we're sorry to disappoint you. There is no encryption in Bitcoin, because nothing needs to be encrypted, as we'll see. Encryption is only one of a rich suite of techniques made possible by modern cryptography. Many of them, such as commitment schemes, involve hiding information in some way, but they are distinct from encryption.

10.3 Public Keys as Identities

Let's look at a nice trick that goes along with digital signatures. The idea is to take a public key, one of those public verification keys from a digital signature scheme, and equate that to an identity of a person or an actor in a system. If you see a message with a signature that verifies correctly under a public key, pk, then you can think of this as pk is saying the message. You can literally think of a public key as kind of like an actor, or a party in a system who can make statements by signing those statements. From this viewpoint, the public key is an identity. In order for someone to speak for the identity pk, they must know the corresponding secret key, sk.

A consequence of treating public keys as identities is that you can make a new identity whenever you want — you simply create a new fresh key pair, sk a nd pk, via the **generateKeys** operation in our digital signature scheme. pk is the new public identity that you can use, and sk is the correspondings e c r e t k e y t h a t o n l y y o u k n o w a n d l e t s y o u s p e a k f o r o n b e h a l f o f t h e i d e n t i t y p k . I n p r a c t i c e , y o u m a y use the hash of pk as your identity since public keys are large. If you do that, then in order to verify that a message comes from your identity, one will have to check (1) that pk indeed hashes to your

i d e n t i t y , a n d (2) t h e m e s s a g e v e r i f i e s u n d e r p u b l i c k e y pk . Moreover, by default, your public key pk will basically look random, and nobody will be able to

4uncover your real world identity by examining pk. You can generate a fresh identity that looks

random, that looks like a face in the crowd, and that only you can control.

Decentralized identity management. T his brings us to the idea of decentralized identity management. Rather than having a central authority that you have to go to in order to register as a user in a system, you can register as a user all by yourself. You don't need to be issued a username nor do you need to

[4] Of course, once you start making statements using this identity, these statements may leak information that allows one to connect pk to your real world identity. We will discuss this in more detail shortly.

inform someone that you're going to be using a particular name. If you want a new identity, you can just generate one at any time, and you can make as many as you want. If you prefer to be known by five different names, no problem! Just make five identities. If you want to be somewhat anonymous for a while, you can make a new identity, use it just for a little while, and then throw it away. All of these things are possible with decentralized identity management, and this is the way Bitcoin, in fact, does identity. These identities are called *a ddresses*, in Bitcoin jargon. You'll frequently hear the term address used in the context of Bitcoin and cryptocurrencies, and that's really just a hash of a public key. It's an identity that someone made up out of thin air, as part of this decentralized identity management scheme.

Sidebar. The idea that you can generate an identity without a centralized authority may seem counterintuitive. After all, if someone else gets lucky and generates the same key as you can't they steal your bitcoins?

The answer is that the probability of someone else generating the same 256-bit key as you is so small that we don't have to worry about it in practice. We are for all intents and purposes guaranteed that it will never happen.

More generally, in contrast to beginners' intuition that probabilistic systems are unpredictable and hard to reason about, often the opposite is true — the theory of statistics allows us to precisely quantify the chances of events we're interested in and make confident assertions about the behavior of such systems.

But there's a subtlety: the probabilistic guarantee is true only when keys are generated at random. The generation of randomness is often a weak point in real systems. If two users' computers use the same source of randomness or use predictable randomness, then the theoretical guarantees no longer apply. So it is crucial to use a good source of randomness when generating keys to ensure that practical guarantees match the theoretical ones.

On first glance, it may seems that decentralized identity management leads to great anonymity and privacy. After all, you can create a random-looking identity all by yourself without telling anyone your real-world identity. But it's not that simple. Over time, the identity that you create makes a series of statements. People see these statements and thus know that whoever owns this identity has done a certain series of actions. They can start to connect the dots, using this series of actions to infer things about your real-world identity. An observer can link together these things over time, and make inferences that lead them to conclusions such as, "Gee, this person is acting a lot like Joe. Maybe this person is Joe."

In other words, in Bitcoin you don't need to explicitly register or reveal your real-world identity, but the pattern of your behavior might itself be identifying. This is the fundamental privacy question in a cryptocurrency like Bitcoin, and indeed we'll devote the entirety of Chapter 6 to it.

10.4 A Simple Cryptocurrency

Now let's move from cryptography to cryptocurrencies. Eating our cryptographic vegetables will start to pay off here, and we'll gradually see how the pieces fit together and why cryptographic operations like hash functions and digital signatures are actually useful. In this section we'll discuss two very simple cryptocurrencies. Of course, it's going to require much of the rest of the book to spell out all the implications of how Bitcoin itself works.

GoofyCoin

The first of the two is GoofyCoin, which is about the simplest cryptocurrency we can imagine. There are just two rules of GoofyCoin. The first rule is that a designated entity, Goofy, can create new coins whenever he wants and these newly created coins belong to him.

To create a coin , Goofy g e n e r a t e s a u n i q u e c o i n I D u n i q u e C o i n I D t h a t h e ' s n e v e r g e n e r a t e d b e f o r e and constructs the string "CreateCoin [uniqueCoinID] ". He then computes the digital signature of this string with his secret signing key. The string, together with Goofy's signature, is a coin. Anyone can verify that the coin contains Goofy's valid signature of a CreateCoin statement, and is therefore a valid coin.

The second rule of GoofyCoin is that whoever owns a coin can transfer it on to someone else. Transferring a coin is not simply a matter of sending the coin data structure to the recipient — it's done using cryptographic operations.

Let's say Goofy wants to transfer a coin that he created to Alice. To do this he creates a new statement that says "Pay this to Alice" where "this" is a hash pointer that references the coin in question. And as we saw earlier, identities are really just public keys, so "Alice" refers to Alice's public key. Finally, Goofy signs the string representing the statement. Since Goofy is the one who originally owned that coin, he has to sign any transaction that spends the coin. Once this data structure representing Goofy's transaction signed by him exists, Alice owns the coin. She can prove to anyone that she owns the coin, because she can present the data structure with Goofy's valid signature. Furthermore, it points to a valid coin that was owned by Goofy. So the validity and ownership of coins are self-evident in the system.

Once Alice owns the coin, she can spend it in turn. To do this she creates a statement that says, "Pay this coin to Bob's public key" where "this" is a hash pointer to the coin that was owned by her. And of course, Alice signs this statement. Anyone, when presented with this coin, can verify that Bob is the owner. They would follow the chain of hash pointers back to the coin's creation and verify that at each step, the rightful owner signed a statement that says "pay this coin to [new owner]".

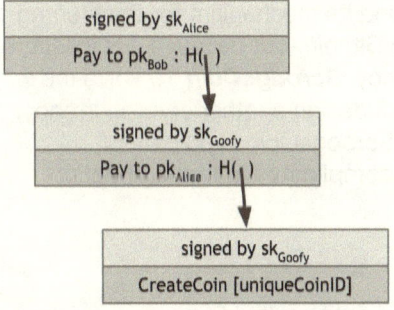

Figure 1.10 GoofyCoin coin. Shown here is a coin that's been created (bottom) and spent twice (middle and top).

To summarize, the rules of GoofyCoin are:

- Goofy can create new coins by simply signing a statement that he's making a new coin with a unique coin ID.

- Whoever owns a coin can pass it on to someone else by signing a statement that saying, "Pass on this coin to X" (where X is specified as a public key)

- Anyone can verify the validity of a coin by following the chain of hash pointers back to its creation by Goofy, verifying all of the signatures along the way. Of course, there's a fundamental security problem with GoofyCoin. Let's say Alice passed her coin on to Bob by sending her signed statement to Bob but didn't tell anyone else. She could create another signed statement that pays the very same coin to Chuck. To Chuck, it would appear that it is perfectly valid transaction, and now he's the owner of the coin. Bob and Chuck would both have valid-looking claims to be the owner of this coin. This is called a double-spending attack — Alice is spending the same coin twice. Intuitively, we know coins are not supposed to work that way. In fact, double-spending attacks are one of the key problems that any cryptocurrency has to solve. GoofyCoin does not solve the double-spending attack and therefore it's not secure. GoofyCoin is simple, and its mechanism for transferring coins is actually very similar to Bitcoin, but because it is insecure it won't cut it as a cryptocurrency. **ScroogeCoin** To solve the double-spending problem, we'll design another cryptocurrency, which we'll call ScroogeCoin. ScroogeCoin is built off of GoofyCoin, but it's a bit more complicated in terms of data structures.

The first key idea is that a designated entity called Scrooge publishes an *a ppend-only l edger* containing the history of all the transactions that have happened. The append-only property ensures that any data written to this ledger will remain forever. If the ledger is truly append-only, we can use it to defend against double-spending by requiring all transactions to be written the ledger before they are accepted. That way, it will be publicly visible if coins were previously sent to a different owner.

To implement this append-only functionality, Scrooge can build a block chain (the data structure we discussed before) which he will digitally sign. It's a series of data blocks, each with one transaction in it (in practice, as an optimization, we'd really put multiple transactions into the same block, as Bitcoin does.) Each block has the ID of a transaction, the transaction's contents, and a hash pointer to the previous block. Scrooge digitally signs the final hash pointer, which binds all of the data in this entire structure, and publishes the signature along with the block chain.

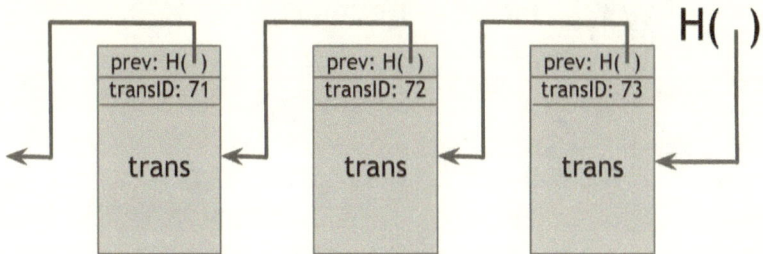

Figure 1.11 ScroogeCoin block chain.

In ScroogeCoin a transaction only counts if it is in the block chain signed by Scrooge. Anybody can verify that a transaction was endorsed by Scrooge by checking Scrooge's signature on the block that it appears in. Scrooge makes sure that he doesn't endorse a transaction that attempts to double-spend an already spent coin.

Why do we need a block chain with hash pointers in addition to having Scrooge sign each block? This ensures the append-only property. If Scrooge tries to add or remove a transaction to the history, or change an existing transaction, it will affect all of the following blocks because of the hash pointers. As long as someone is monitoring the latest hash pointer published by Scrooge, the change will be obvious and easy to catch. In a system where Scrooge signed blocks individually, you'd have to keep track of every single signature Scrooge ever issued. A block chain makes it very easy for any two individuals to verify that they have observed the exact same history of transactions signed by Scrooge.

In ScroogeCoin, there are two kinds of transactions. The first kind is CreateCoins, which is just like the operation Goofy could do in GoofyCoin that makes a new coin. With ScroogeCoin, we'll extend the semantics a bit to allow multiple coins to be created in one transaction.

transID: 73		type:CreateCoins
coins created		
num	value	recipient
0	3.2	0x...	← coinID 73(0)
1	1.4	0x...	← coinID 73(1)
2	7.1	0x...	← coinID 73(2)

Figure 1.12 CreateCoins transaction. This CreateCoins transaction creates multiple coins. Each coin has a serial number within the transaction. Each coin also has a value; it's worth a certain number of scroogecoins. Finally, each coin has a recipient, which is a public key that gets the coin when it's created. So CreateCoins creates a bunch of new coins with different values and assigns them to people as initial owners. We refer to coins by CoinIDs. A CoinID is a combination of a transaction ID and the coin's serial number within that transaction. A CreateCoins transaction is always valid by definition if it is signed by Scrooge. We won't worry about when Scrooge is entitled to create coins or how many, just like we didn't worry in GoofyCoin about how

Goofy is chosen as the entity allowed to create coins.

The second kind of transaction is PayCoins. It consumes some coins, that is, destroys them, and creates new coins of the same total value. The new coins might belong to different people (public keys). This transaction has to be signed by everyone who's paying in a coin. So if you're the owner of one of the coins that's going to be consumed in this transaction, then you need to digitally sign the transaction to say that you're really okay with spending this coin.

The rules of ScroogeCoin say that PayCoins transaction is valid if four things are true:

- The consumed coins are valid, that is, they really were created in previous transactions.

- The consumed coins were not already consumed in some previous transaction. That is, that this is not a double-spend.

- The total value of the coins that come out of this transaction is equal to the total value of the coins that went in. That is, only Scrooge can create new value.

- The transaction is validly signed by the owners of all of the consumed coins.

transID: 73		type:PayCoins
consumed coinIDs: 68(1), 42(0), 72(3)		
coins created		
num	value	recipient
0	3.2	0x...
1	1.4	0x...
2	7.1	0x...
signatures		

Figure 1 .13 A PayCoins Transaction.

If all of those conditions are met, then this PayCoins transaction is valid and Scrooge will accept it. He'll write it into the history by appending it to the block chain, after which everyone can see that this transaction has happened. It is only at this point that the participants can accept that the transaction has actually occurred. Until it is published, it might be preempted by a double-spending transaction even if it is otherwise valid by the first three conditions.

Coins in this system are immutable — they are never changed, subdivided, or combined. Each coin is created, once, in one transaction and later consumed in some other transaction. But we can get the same effect as being able to subdivide or combine coins by using transactions. For example, to subdivide a coin, Alice create a new transaction that consumes that one coin, and then produces two new coins of the same total value. Those two new coins could be assigned back to her. So although coins are immutable in this system, it has all the flexibility of a system that didn't have immutable coins.

Now, we come to the core problem with ScroogeCoin. ScroogeCoin will work in the sense that people can see which coins are valid. It prevents double-spending, because everyone can look into the block chain and see that all of the transactions are valid and that every coin is consumed only once. But the problem is Scrooge — he has too much influence. He can't create fake transactions, because he can't forge other people's signatures. But he could stop endorsing transactions from some users, denying them service and making their coins unspendable. If Scrooge is greedy (as his cartoon namesake suggests) he could refuse to publish transactions unless they transfer some mandated transaction fee to him. Scrooge can also of course create as many new coins for himself as he wants. Or Scrooge could get bored of the whole system and stop updating the block chain completely.

The problem here is centralization. Although Scrooge is happy with this system, we, as users of it, might not be. While ScroogeCoin may seem like an unrealistic proposal, much of the early research on cryptosystems assumed there would indeed be some central trusted authority, typically referred to as a bank. After all, most real-world currencies do have a trusted issuer (typically a government mint) responsible for creating currency and determining which notes are valid. However, cryptocurrencies with a central authority largely failed to take off in practice. There are many reasons for this, but in hindsight it appears that it's difficult to get people to accept a cryptocurrency with a centralized authority.

Therefore, the central technical challenge that we need to solve in order to improve on ScroogeCoin and create a workable system is: can we descroogify the system? That is, can we get rid of that centralized Scrooge figure? Can we have a cryptocurrency that operates like ScroogeCoin in many ways, but doesn't have any central trusted authority?

To do that, we need to figure out how all users can agree upon a single published block chain as the history of which transactions have happened. They must all agree on which transactions are valid, and which transactions have actually occurred. They also need to be able to assign IDs to things in a decentralized way. Finally, the minting of new coins needs to be controlled in a decentralized way. If we can solve all of those problems, then we can build a currency that would be like ScroogeCoin but without a centralized party. In fact, this would be a system very much like Bitcoin.

11 HOW BITCOIN ACHIEVES DECENTRALIZATION

In this chapter, we will discuss decentralization in Bitcoin. In the first chapter we looked at the crypto basics that underlie Bitcoin and we ended with a simple currency that we called ScroogeCoin. ScroogeCoin achieves a lot of what we want in a ledger-based cryptocurrency, but it has one glaring problem — it relies upon the centralized authority called Scrooge. We ended with the question of how to decentralize, or de-Scrooge-ify, this currency, and answering that question will be the focus of this chapter.

As you read through this chapter, take note that the mechanism through which Bitcoin achieves decentralization is not purely technical, but it's a combination of technical methods and clever incentive engineering. At the end of this chapter you should have a really good appreciation for how this decentralization happens, and more generally how Bitcoin works and why it is secure.

11.1 Centralization vs. Decentralization

Decentralization is an important concept that is not unique to Bitcoin. The notion of competing paradigms of centralization versus decentralization arises in a variety of different digital technologies. In order to best understand how it plays out in Bitcoin, it is useful to understand the central conflict — the tension between these two paradigms — in a variety of other contexts.

On the one hand we have the Internet, a famously decentralized system that has historically competed with and prevailed against "walled-garden" alternatives like AOL's and CompuServe's information services. Then there's email, which at its core is a decentralized system based on the Simple Mail Transfer Protocol (SMTP), an open standard. While it does have competition from proprietary messaging systems like Facebook or LinkedIn mail, email has managed to remain the default for person-to-person communication online. In the case of instant messaging and text messaging, we have a hybrid model that can't be categorically described as centralized or decentralized. Finally there's social networking: despite numerous concerted efforts by hobbyists, developers and entrepreneurs to create alternatives to the dominant centralized model, centralized systems like Facebook and LinkedIn still dominate this space. In fact, this conflict long predates the digital era and we see a similar struggle between the two models in the history of telephony, radio, television, and film.

Decentralization is not all or nothing; almost no system is purely decentralized or purely centralized. For example, email is fundamentally a decentralized system based on a standardized protocol, SMTP, and anyone who wishes can operate an email server of their own. Yet, what has happened in the market is that a small number of centralized webmail providers have become dominant. Similarly, while the Bitcoin protocol is decentralized, services like Bitcoin exchanges, where you can convert

Bitcoin into other currencies, and wallet software, or software that allows people to manage their bitcoins may be centralized or decentralized to varying degrees.

With this in mind, let's break down the question of how the Bitcoin protocol achieves decentralization into five more specific questions:

1. Who maintains the ledger of transactions?

2. Who has authority over which transactions are valid?

3. Who creates new bitcoins?

4. Who determines how the rules of the system change?

5. How do bitcoins acquire exchange value?

The first three questions reflect the technical details of the Bitcoin protocol, and it is these questions that will be the focus of this chapter.

Different aspects of Bitcoin fall on different points on the centralization/decentralization spectrum. The peer-to-peer network is close to purely decentralized since anybody can run a Bitcoin node and there's a fairly low barrier to entry. You can go online and easily download a Bitcoin client and run a node on your laptop or your PC. Currently there are several thousand such nodes. Bitcoin *m ining*, which we'll study later in this chapter, is technically also open to anyone, but it requires a very high capital cost. Because of this there has been a high degree of centralization, or a concentration of power, in the Bitcoin mining ecosystem. Many in the Bitcoin community see this as quite undesirable. A third aspect is updates to the software that Bitcoin nodes run, and this has a bearing on how and when the rules of the system change. One can imagine that there are numerous interoperable implementations of the protocol, as with email. But in practice, most nodes run the reference implementation, and its developers are trusted by the community and have a lot of power.

11.2 Distributed Consensus

We've discussed, in a generic manner, centralization and decentralization. Let's now examine decentralization in Bitcoin at a more technical level. A key term that will come up throughout this discussion is *c onsensus*, and specifically, ***distributed consensus***. The key technical problem to solve in building a distributed e-cash system is achieving distributed consensus. Intuitively, you can think of our goal as decentralizing ScroogeCoin, the hypothetical currency that we saw in the first chapter.

Distributed consensus has various applications, and it has been studied for decades in computer science. The traditional motivating application is reliability in distributed systems. Imagine you're in charge of the backend for a large social networking company like Facebook. Systems of this sort typically have thousands or even millions of servers, which together form a massive distributed database that records all of the actions that happen in the system. Each piece of information must be recorded on several different nodes in this backend, and the nodes must be in sync about the overall state of the system.

The implications of having a distributed consensus protocol reach far beyond this traditional application. If we had such a protocol, we could use it to build a massive, distributed key-value store, that maps arbitrary keys, or names, to arbitrary values. A distributed key-value store, in turn, would enable many applications. For example, we could use it to build a distributive domain name system, which is simply a mapping between human understandable domain names to IP addresses. We could build a public key directory, which is a mapping between email addresses (or some other form of real-world identity) to public keys.

That's the intuition of what distributed consensus is, but it is useful to provide a technical definition as this will help us determine whether or not a given protocol meets the requirements.

What does this mean in the context of Bitcoin? To understand how distributed consensus could work in Bitcoin, remember that Bitcoin is a peer-to-peer system. When Alice wants to pay Bob, what she actually does is broadcast a transaction to all of the Bitcoin nodes that comprise the peer-to-peer network. See Figure 2.1.

Figure 2.1 Broadcasting a transaction In order to pay Bob, Alice broadcasts the transaction to the entire Bitcoin peer-to-peer network.

Incidentally, you may have noticed that Alice broadcasts the transaction to all the Bitcoin peer-to-peer nodes, but Bob's computer is nowhere in this picture. It's of course possible that Bob is running one of the nodes in the peer-to-peer network. In fact, if he wants to be notified that this transaction did in fact happen and that he got paid, running a node might be a good idea. Nevertheless, there is no requirement that Bob be listening on the network; running a node is not necessary for Bob to receive the funds. The bitcoins will be his whether or not he's operating a node on the network.

What exactly is it that the nodes might want to reach consensus on in the Bitcoin network? Given that a variety of users are broadcasting these transactions to the network, the nodes must agree on

Distributed consensus protocol. T here are *n* n odes that each have an input value. Some of these nodes a re faulty or malicious. A distributed consensus protocol has the following two properties:

- It must terminate with all honest nodes in agreement on the value

- The value must have been generated by an honest node

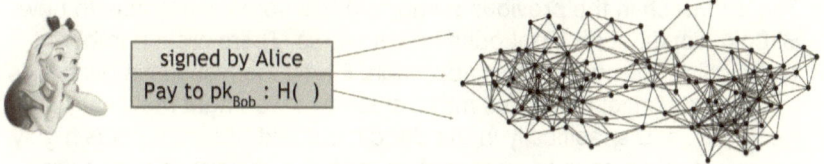

exactly which transactions were broadcast and the order in which these transactions happened. This will result in a single, global ledger for the system. Recall that in ScroogeCoin, for optimization, we put transactions into blocks. Similarly, in Bitcoin, we do consensus on a block-by-block basis.

So at any given point, all the nodes in the peer-to-peer network have a ledger consisting of a sequence of blocks, each containing a list of transactions, that they've reached consensus on. Additionally, each node has a pool of outstanding transactions that it has heard about but have not yet been included on the block chain. For these transactions, consensus has not yet happened, and so by definition, each node might have a slightly different version of the outstanding transaction pool. In practice, this occurs because the peer-to-peer network is not perfect, so some nodes may have heard about a transaction that other nodes have not heard about.

How exactly do nodes come to consensus on a block? One way to do this: at regular intervals, say every 10 minutes, every node in the system proposes its own outstanding transaction pool to be the next block. Then the nodes execute some consensus protocol, where each node's input is its own proposed block. Now, some nodes may be malicious and put invalid transactions into their blocks, but we might assume that other nodes will be honest. If the consensus protocol succeeds, a valid block will be selected as the output. Even if the selected block was proposed by only one node, it's a valid output as long as the block is valid. Now there may be some valid outstanding transaction that did not get included in the block, but this is not a problem. If some transaction somehow didn't make it into this particular block, it could just wait and get into the next block.

The approach in the previous paragraph has some similarities to how Bitcoin works, but it's not quite how it works. There are a number of technical problems with this approach. Firstly, consensus in general is a hard problem since nodes might crash or be outright malicious. Secondly, and specifically in the Bitcoin context, the network is highly imperfect. It's a peer-to-peer system, and not all pairs of nodes are connected to each other. There could be faults in the network because of poor Internet connectivity for example, and thus running a consensus protocol in which all nodes must participate is not really possible. Finally, there's a lot of latency in the system because it's distributed all over the Internet.

Sidebar: The Bitcoin protocol must reach consensus in the face of two types of obstacles: imperfections in the network, such as latency and nodes crashing, as well as deliberate attempts by some nodes to subvert the process.

One particular consequence of this high latency is that there is no notion of global time. What this means is that not all nodes can agree to a common ordering of events simply based on observing timestamps. So the consensus protocol cannot contain instructions of the form, "The node that sent the first message in step 1 must do X in step 2." This simply will not work because not all nodes will agree on which message was sent first in the step 1 of the protocol.

Impossibility results. T he lack of global time heavily constrains the set of algorithms that can be used in the consensus protocols. In fact, because of these constraints, much of the literature on distributed consensus is somewhat pessimistic, and many impossibility results have been proven. One very well known impossibility result concerns the **Byzantine Generals Problem**. In this classic problem, the Byzantine army is separated into divisions, each commanded by a general. The generals communicate by messenger in order to devise a joint plan of action. Some generals may be traitors and may intentionally try to subvert the process so that the loyal generals cannot arrive at a unified plan. The goal of this problem is for all of the loyal generals to arrive at the same plan without the traitorous generals being able to cause them to adopt a bad plan. It has been proven that this is impossible to achieve if one-third or more of the generals are traitors.

A much more subtle impossibility result, known for the names of the authors who first proved it, is called the Fischer-Lynch-Paterson impossibility result. Under some conditions, which include the nodes acting in a deterministic manner, they proved that consensus is impossible with even a single faulty process.

Despite these impossibility results, there are some consensus protocols in the literature. One of the better known among these protocols is **Paxos**. Paxos makes certain compromises. On the one hand, it never produces an inconsistent result. On the other hand, it accepts the trade-off that under certain conditions, albeit rare ones, the protocol can get stuck and fail to make any progress.

Breaking traditional assumptions. B ut there's good news: these impossibility results were proven in a very specific model. They were intended to study distributed databases, and this model doesn't carry over very well to the Bitcoin setting because Bitcoin violates many of the assumptions built into the models. In a way, the results tell us more about the model than they do about the problem of distributed consensus.

Ironically, with the current state of research, consensus in Bitcoin works better in practice than in theory. That is, we observe consensus working, but have not developed the theory to fully explain why it works. But developing such a theory is important as it can help us predict unforeseen attacks and problems, and only when we have a strong theoretical understanding of how Bitcoin consensus works will we have strong guarantees Bitcoin's security and stability.

What are the assumptions in traditional models for consensus that Bitcoin violates? First, it introduces the idea of incentives, which is novel for a distributed consensus protocol. This is only possible in Bitcoin because it is a currency and therefore has a natural mechanism to incentivize participants to act honestly. So Bitcoin doesn't quite solve the distributed consensus problem in a general sense, but it solves it in the specific context of a currency system.

Second, Bitcoin embraces the notion of randomness. As we will see in the next two sections, Bitcoin's consensus algorithm relies heavily on randomization. Also, it does away with the notion of a specific starting point and ending point for consensus. Instead, consensus happens over a long period of time, about an hour in the practical system. But even at the end of that time, nodes can't be certain that any particular transaction or a block has made it into the ledger. Instead, as time goes on, the probability that your view of any block will match the eventual consensus view increases, and the probability that the views will diverge goes down exponentially. These differences in the model are key to how Bitcoin gets around the traditional impossibility results for distributed consensus protocols.

11.3 Consensus Without Identity Using A Block Chain

In this section we'll study the technical details of Bitcoin's consensus algorithm. Recall that Bitcoin nodes do not have persistent, long-term identities. This is another difference from traditional distributed consensus algorithms. One reason for this lack of identities is that in a peer-to-peer system, there is no central authority to assign identities to participants and verify that they're not creating new nodes at will . The technical term for this is a **Sbil attack** . Sybils are just copies of nodes that a malicious adversary can create to look like there are a lot of different participants, when in fact all those pseudo-participants are really controlled by the same adversary. The other reason is that pseudonymity is inherently a goal of Bitcoin. Even if it were possible or easy to establish identities for all nodes or all participants, we wouldn't necessarily want to do that. Although Bitcoin doesn't give strong anonymity guarantees in that the different transactions that one makes can often be linked together, it does have the property that nobody is forced to reveal their real-life identity, like their name or IP address, in order to participate. And that's an important property and a central feature of Bitcoin's design.

If nodes did have identities, the design would be easier. For starters, identities would allow us to put in the protocol instructions of the form, "Now the node with the lowest numerical ID should take some step." Without identities, the set of possible instructions is more constrained. But a much more serious reason for nodes to have identities is for security. If nodes were identified and it weren't trivial to create new node identities, then we could make assumptions on the number of nodes that are malicious, and we could derive security properties out of that. For both of these reasons, the lack of identities introduces difficulties for the consensus protocol in Bitcoin.

We can compensate for the lack of identities by making a weaker assumption. Suppose there is somehow an ability to pick a random node in the system. A good motivating analogy for this is a lottery or a raffle, or any number of real-life systems where it's hard to track people, give them identities and verify those identities. What we do in those contexts is to give out tokens or tickets or something similar. That enables us to later pick a random token ID, and call upon the owner of that ID. So for the moment, take a leap of faith and assume that it is possible to pick a random node from the Bitcoin network in this manner. Further assume, for the moment, that this token generation and distribution algorithm is sufficiently smart so that if the adversary is going to try to create a lot of Sybil nodes, all of those Sybils together will get only one token. This means the adversary is not able to multiply his power by creating new nodes. If you think this is a lot to assume, don't worry. Later in this chapter, we'll remove these assumptions and show in detail how properties equivalent to these are realized in Bitcoin.

Implicit Consensus. This assumption of random node selection makes possible something called ***implicit consensus***. There are multiple rounds in our protocol, each corresponding to a different block in the block chain. In each round, a random node is somehow selected, and this node gets to propose the next block in the chain. There is no consensus algorithm for selecting the block, and no voting of any kind. The chosen node unilaterally proposes what the next block in the block chain will be. But what if that node is malicious? Well, there is a process for handling that, but it is an implicit one. Other nodes will implicitly accept or reject that block by choosing whether or not to build on top of it. If they accept that block, they will signal their acceptance by extending the block chain including the accepted block. By contrast, if they reject that block, they will extend the chain by ignoring that block, and building on top of whichever is the previous block that they accepted. Recall that each block contains a hash of the block that it extends. This is the technical mechanism that allows nodes to signal which block it is that they are extending.

Bitcoin consensus algorithm (simplified)

This algorithm is simplified in that it assumes the ability to select a random node in a manner that is not vulnerable to Sybil attacks.

1. New transactions are broadcast to all nodes

2. Each node collects new transactions into a block

3. In each round a random node gets to broadcast its block

4. Other nodes accept the block only if all transactions in it are valid (unspent, valid signatures)

5. Nodes express their acceptance of the block by including its hash in the next block they create

――――

Let's now try to understand why this consensus algorithm works. To do this, let's consider how a malicious adversary — who we'll call Alice — may be able to subvert this process.

Stealing Bitcoins. C an Alice simply steal bitcoins belonging to another user at an address she doesn't control? No. Even if it is Alice's turn to propose the next block in the chain, she cannot steal other users' bitcoins. Doing so would require Alice to create a valid transaction that spends that coin. This would require Alice to forge the owners' signatures which she cannot do if a secure digital signature scheme is used. So as long as the underlying cryptography is solid, she's not able to simply steal bitcoins.

Denial of service attack. L et's consider another attack. Say Alice really dislikes some other user Bob. Alice can then decide that she will not include any transactions originating from Bob's address in any block that she proposes to get onto the block chain. In other words, she's denying service to Bob. While this is a valid attack that Alice can try to mount, luckily it's nothing more than a minor

annoyance. If Bob's transaction doesn't make it into the next block that Alice proposes, he will just wait until an honest node gets the chance to propose a block and then his transaction will get into that block. So that's not really a good attack either.

Double-spend attack. A lice may try to launch a double-spend attack. To understand how that works, let's assume that Alice is a customer of some online merchant or website run by Bob, who provides some online service in exchange for payment in bitcoins. Let's say Bob's service allows the download of some software. So here's how a double-spend attack might work. Alice adds an item to her shopping cart on Bob's website and the server requests payment. Then Alice creates a Bitcoin transaction from her address to Bob's and broadcasts it to the network. Let's say that some honest node creates the next block, and includes this transaction in that block. So there is now a block that was created by an honest node that contains a transaction that represents a payment from Alice to the merchant Bob.

Recall that a transaction is a data structure that contains Alice's signature, an instruction to pay to Bob's public key, and a hash. This hash represents a pointer to a previous transaction output that Alice received and is now spending. That pointer must reference a transaction that was included in some previous block in the consensus chain.

Note, by the way, that there are two different types of hash pointers here that can easily be confused. Blocks include a hash pointer to the previous block that they're extending. Transactions include one or more hash pointers to previous transaction outputs that are being redeemed.

Let's return to how Alice can launch a double spend attack. The latest block was generated by an honest node and includes a transaction in which Alice pays Bob for the software download. Upon seeing this transaction included in the block chain, Bob concludes that Alice has paid him and allows Alice to download the software. Suppose the next random node that is selected in the next round happens to be controlled by Alice. Now since Alice gets to propose the next block, she could propose a block that ignores the block that contains the payment to Bob and instead contains a pointer to the previous block. Furthermore, in the block that she proposes, Alice includes a transaction that transfers the very coins that she was sending to Bob to a different address that she herself controls. This is a classic double-spend pattern. Since the two transactions spend the same coins, only one of them can be included in the block chain. If Alice succeeds in including the payment to her own address in the block chain, then the transaction in which she pays Bob is useless as it can never be included later in the block chain.

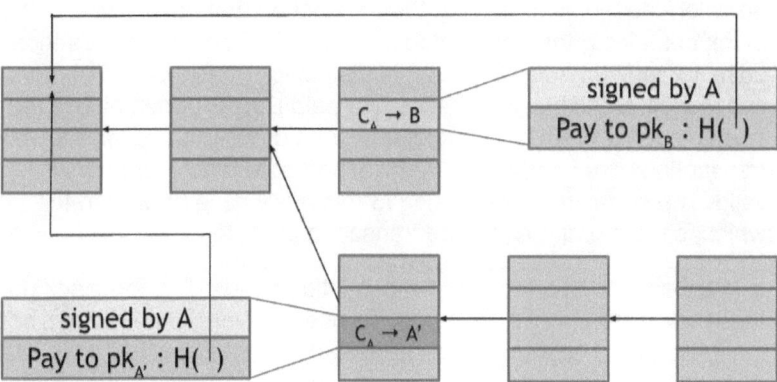

Figure 2.2 A double spend attempt. A lice creates two transactions: one in which she sends Bob Bitcoins, and a second in which she double spends those Bitcoins by sending them to a different address that she controls. As they spend the same Bitcoins, only one of these transactions can be included in the block chain. T he arrows are pointers from one block to the previous block that it extends including a hash of that previous block within its own contents. C_A is used to denote a coin owned by Alice.

And how do we know if this double spend attempt is going to succeed or not? Well, that depends on which block will ultimately end up on the long-term consensus chain — the one with the Alice → Bob transaction or the one with the Alice → Alice transaction. What determines which block will be included? I lonest nodes follow the policy of extending the longest valid branch, so which branch will they extend? There is no right answer! At this point, the two branches are the same length — they only differ in the last block and both of these blocks are valid. The node that chooses the next block then may decide to build upon either one of them, and this choice will largely determine whether or not the double-spend succeeds.

A subtle point: from a moral point of view, there is a clear difference between the block containing the transaction that pays Bob and the block containing the transaction in which Alice double spends those coins to her own address. But this distinction is only based on our knowledge of the story that Alice first paid Bob and then attempted to double spend. From a technological point of view, however, these two transactions are completely identical and both blocks are equally valid. The nodes that are looking at this really have no way to tell which is the morally legitimate transaction.

In practice, nodes often follow a heuristic of extending the block that they first heard about on the peer-to-peer network. But it's not a solid rule. And in any case, because of network latency, it could easily be that the block that a node first heard about is actually the one that was created second. So there is at least some chance that the next node that gets to propose a block will extend the block containing the double spend. Alice could further try to increase the likelihood of this happening by bribing the next node to do so. If the next node does build on the double-spend block for whatever reason, then this chain will now be longer than the one that includes the transaction to Bob. At this

point, the next honest node is much more likely to continue to build on this chain since it is longer. This process will continue, and it will become increasingly likely that the block containing the double-spend will be part of the long-term consensus chain. The block containing the transaction to Bob, on the other hand, gets completely ignored by the network, and this is now called an **orphan block**.

Let's now reconsider this whole situation from Bob-the-merchant's point of view. Understanding how Bob can protect himself from this double-spending attack is a key part of understanding Bitcoin security. When Alice broadcasts the transaction that represents her payment to Bob, Bob is listening on the network and hears about this transaction even before the next block is created. If Bob was even more foolhardy than we previously described, he can complete the checkout process on the website and allow Alice to download the software right at that moment. That's called a **zero-confirmation transaction**. This leads to an even more basic double spend attack than the one described before. Previously, for the double-spend attack to occur, we had to assume that a malicious actor controls the node that proposes the next block. But if Bob allows Alice to download the software before the transaction receives even a single confirmation on the block chain, then Alice can immediately broadcast a double-spend transaction, and an honest node may include it in the next block instead of the transaction that pays Bob.

Figure 2.3 Bob the Merchant's view. This is what Alice's double-spend attempt looks like from Bob the merchant's viewpoint. In order to protect himself from this attack, Bob should wait until the transaction with which Alice pays him is included in the block chain and has several confirmations.

On the other hand, a cautious merchant would not release the software to Alice even after the transaction was included in one block, and would continue to wait. If Bob sees that Alice successfully launches a double-spend attack, he realizes that the block containing Alice's payment to him has been orphaned. He should abandon the transaction and not let Alice download the software. Instead, if it happens that despite the double-spend attempt, the next several nodes build on the block with the Alice → Bob transaction, then Bob gains confidence that this transaction will be on the long-term consensus chain.

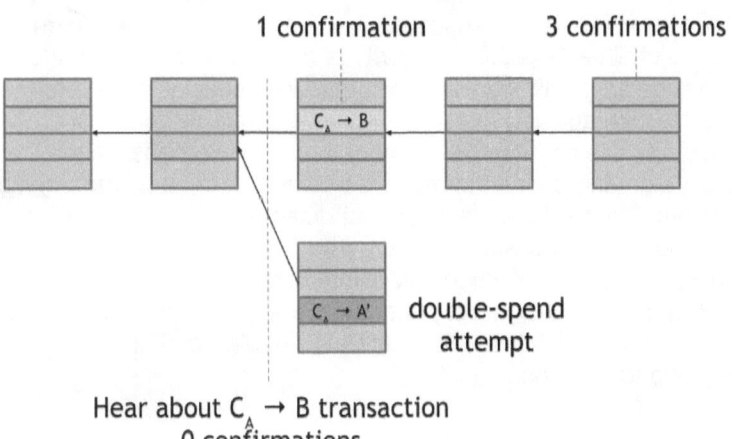

1 confirmation   3 confirmations

$C_A \to B$

$C_A \to A'$ double-spend attempt

Hear about $C_A \to B$ transaction
0 confirmations

In general, the more confirmations a transaction gets, the higher the probability that it is going to end up on the long-term consensus chain. Recall that honest nodes' behavior is always to extend the longest valid branch that they see. The chance that the shorter branch with the double spend will catch up to the longer branch becomes increasingly tiny as it grows longer than any other branch. This is especially true if only a minority of the nodes are malicious — for a shorter branch to catch up, several malicious nodes would have to be picked in close succession.

In fact, the double-spend probability decreases exponentially with the number of confirmations. So, if the transaction that you're interested in has received k c onfirmations, then the probability that a double-spend transaction will end up on the long-term consensus chain goes down exponentially as a function of k . The most common heuristic that's used in the Bitcoin ecosystem is to wait for six confirmations. There is nothing really special about the number six. It's just a good tradeoff between the amount of time you have to wait and your guarantee that the transaction you're interested in ends up on the consensus block chain.

To recap, protection against invalid transactions is entirely cryptographic. But it is enforced by consensus, which means that if a node does attempt to include a cryptographically invalid transaction, then the only reason that transaction won't end up in the long-term consensus chain is because a majority of the nodes are honest and won't include an invalid transaction in the block chain. On the other hand, protection against double-spending is purely by consensus. Cryptography has nothing to say about this, and two transactions that represent a double-spend attempt are both valid from a cryptographic perspective. But it's the consensus that determines which one will end up on the long-term consensus chain. And finally, you're never 100 percent sure that a transaction you're interested in is on the consensus branch. But, this exponential probability guarantee is rather good. After about six transactions, there's virtually no chance that you're going to go wrong.

11.4 Incentives and proof of work

In the previous section, we got a basic look at Bitcoin's consensus algorithm and a good intuition for why we believe that it's secure. But recall from the beginning of the chapter that Bitcoin's decentralization is partly a technical mechanism and partly clever incentive engineering. So far we've mostly looked at the technical mechanism. Now let's talk about the incentive engineering that happens in Bitcoin.

We asked you to take a leap of faith earlier in assuming that we're able to pick a random node and, perhaps more problematically, that at least 50 percent of the time, this process will pick an honest node. This assumption of honesty is particularly problematic if there are financial incentives for participants to subvert the process, in which case we can't really assume that a node will be honest. The question then becomes: can we give nodes an incentive for behaving honestly?

Consider again the double-spend attempt after one confirmation (Figure 2.3). Can we penalize, somehow, the node that created the block with the double-spend transaction? Well, not really. As we mentioned earlier, it's hard to know which is the morally legitimate transaction. But even if we did, it's still hard to punish nodes since they don't have identities. So instead, let's flip the question around and ask, can we reward each of the nodes that created the blocks that did end up on the long-term consensus chain? Well, again, since those nodes don't reveal their real-world identities, we can't quite mail them cash to their home addresses. If only there were some sort of digital currency that we could use instead... you can probably see where this is going. We're going to use bitcoins to incentivize the nodes that created these blocks.

Let's pause for a moment. Everything that we've described so far is just an abstract algorithm for achieving distributed consensus and is not specific to the application. Now we're going to break out of that model, and we're going to use the fact that the application we're building through this distributed consensus process is in fact a currency. Specifically, we're going to incentivize nodes to behave honestly by paying them in units of this currency.

Block Reward. H ow is this done? There are two separate incentive mechanisms in Bitcoin. The first is the *b lock reward*. According to

BITCOIN OFFLINE VAULT WALLET – BA.NET

the rules of Bitcoin, the node that creates a block gets to include a special transaction in that block. This transaction is a coin-creation transaction, analogous to CreateCoins in Scroogecoin, and the node can also choose the recipient address of this transaction. Of course that node will typically choose an address belonging to itself. You can think of this as a payment to the node in exchange for the service of creating a block on the consensus chain.

At the time of this writing, the value of the block reward is fixed at 25 Bitcoins. But it actually halves every 210,000 blocks. Based on the rate of block creation that we will see shortly, this means that the rate drops roughly every four years. We're now in the second period. For the first four years of Bitcoin's existence, the block reward was 50 bitcoins; now it's 25. And it's going to keep halving. This has some interesting consequences, which we will see shortly.

You may be wondering why the block reward incentivizes honest behavior. It may appear, based on what what we've said so far, that this node gets the block reward regardless of whether it proposes a valid block or behaves maliciously. But this is not true! Think about it — how will this node "collect" its reward? That will only happen if the block in question ends up on the long-term consensus branch because just like every other transaction, the coin-creation transaction will only be accepted by other nodes if it ends up on the consensus chain. That's the key idea behind this incentive mechanism. It's a very subtle but very powerful trick. It incentivizes nodes to behave in whatever way they believe will get other nodes to extend their blocks. So if most of the network is following the longest valid branch rule, it incentivizes all nodes to continue to follow that rule. That's Bitcoin's first incentive mechanism.

We mentioned that every 210,000 blocks (or approximately four years), the block reward is cut in half. In Figure 2.4, the slope of this curve is going to keep halving. This is a geometric series, and you might know that it means that there is a finite sum. It works out to a total of 21 million bitcoins.

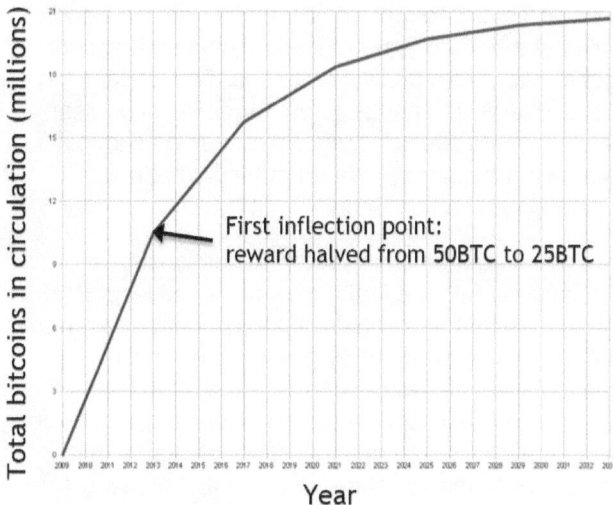

Figure 2.4 The block reward is cut in half every four years limiting the total supply of bitcoins to 21 million.

It is important to note that this is the only way in which new bitcoins are allowed to be created. There is no other coin generation mechanism, and that's why 21 million is a final and total number (as the rules stand now, at least) for how many bitcoins there can ever be. This new block creation reward is actually going to run out in 2140, as things stand now. Does that mean that the system will stop working in 2140 and become insecure because nodes no longer have the incentive to behave honestly? Not quite. The block reward is only the first of two incentive mechanisms in Bitcoin.

Transaction fees The second incentive mechanism is called the **t ransaction fee**. The creator of any transaction can choose to make the total value of the transaction outputs less than the total value of its inputs. Whoever creates the block that first puts that transaction into the block chain gets to collect the difference, which acts a transaction fee. So if you're a node that's creating a block that contains, say, 200 transactions, then the sum of all those 200 transaction fees is paid to the address that you put into that block. The transaction fee is purely voluntary, but we expect, based on our understanding of the system, that as the block reward starts to run out, it will become more and more important, almost mandatory, for users to include transaction fees in order to get a reasonable quality of service. To a certain degree, this is already starting to happen now. But it is yet unclear precisely how the system will evolve; it really depends on a lot of game theory which hasn't been fully worked out yet. That's an interesting area of open research in Bitcoin.

There are still a few problems remaining with the consensus mechanism as we described it. The first major one is the leap of faith that we asked you to take that somehow we can pick a random node. Second, we've created a new problem by giving nodes these incentives for participation. The system can become unstable as the incentives cause a free-for-all where everybody wants to run a Bitcoin node in the hope of capturing some of these rewards. And a third one is an even trickier version of this problem, which is that an adversary might create a large number of Sybil nodes to try and subvert the consensus process.

Mining and proof-of-work. I t turns out that all of these problems are related, and all of them have the same solution, which is called ***p roof-of-work***. The key idea behind proof-of-work is that we approximate the selection of a random node by instead selecting nodes in proportion to a resource that we hope that nobody can monopolize. If, for example, that resource is computing power, then it's a proof-of-work system. Alternately, it could be in proportion to ownership of the currency, and that's called ***p roof-of-stake***. Although it's not used in Bitcoin, proof-of-stake is a legitimate alternate model and it's used in other cryptocurrencies. We'll see more about proof-of-stake and other proof-of-work variants in Chapter 8.

But back to proof-of-work. Let's try to get a better idea of what it means to select nodes in proportion to their computing power. Another way of understanding this is that we're allowing nodes to compete with each other by using their computing power, and that will result in nodes automatically being picked in that proportion. Yet another view of proof-of-work is that we're making it moderately hard to create new identities. It's sort of a tax on identity creation and therefore on the Sybil attack. This might all appear a bit vague, so let's go ahead and look at the details of the proof-of-work system that's used in Bitcoin, which should make things a lot clearer.

Bitcoin achieves proof-of-work using **h ash puzzles**. In order to create a block, the node that proposes that block is required to find a number, or **n once**, such that when you concatenate the nonce, the previous hash, and the list of transactions that comprise that block and take the hash of this whole string, then that hash output should be a number that falls into a target space that is quite small in relation to the much larger output space of that hash function. We can define such a target space as any value falling below a certain target value. In this case, the nonce will have to satisfy the following inequality:

$H(nonce \parallel prev\_hash \parallel tx \parallel tx \parallel ... \parallel tx) < target$

As we saw earlier, normally a block contains a series of transactions that a node is proposing. In addition, a block also contains a hash pointer to the previous block[1]. In addition, we're now requiring that a block also contain a nonce. The idea is that we want to make it moderately difficult to find a nonce that satisfies this required property, which is that hashing the whole block together, including that nonce, is going to result in a particular type of output. If the hash function satisfies the

puzzle-friendliness property from Chapter 1, then the only way to succeed in solving this hash puzzle is to just try enough nonces one by one until you get lucky. So specifically, if this target space were just one percent of the overall output space, you would have to try about 100 nonces before you got lucky. In reality, the size of this target space is not nearly as high as one percent of the output space. It's much, much smaller than that as we will see shortly.

This notion of hash puzzles and proof of work completely does away with the requirement to magically pick a random node. Instead, nodes are simply independently competing to solve these hash puzzles all the time. Once in a while, one of them will get lucky and will find a random nonce that satisfies this property. That lucky node then gets to propose the next block. That's how the system is completely decentralized. There is nobody deciding which node it is that gets to propose the next block.

Difficult to compute. There are three important properties of hash puzzles. The first is that they need to be quite difficult to compute. We said moderately difficult, but you'll see why this actually varies

20 with time. As of the end of 2014, the difficulty level is about 10 hashes per block. In other words the

20 size of the target space is only 1/10 of the size of the output space of the hash function. This is a lot

of computation — it's out of the realm of possibility for a commodity laptop, for example. Because of this, only some nodes even bother to compete in this block creation process. This process of repeated ly trying and solving these hash puzzles is known as **Bitcoinmining**, and we call the participating nodes **miners**. Even though technically anybody can be a miner, there's been a lot of concentration of power in the mining ecosystem due to the high cost of mining.

Parameterizable cost. The second property is that we want the cost to be parameterizable, not a fixed cost for all time. The way that's accomplished is that all the nodes in the Bitcoin peer-to-peer network will automatically recalculate the target, that is the size of the target space as a fraction of the output space, every 2016 blocks. They recalculate the target in such a way that the average time between successive blocks produced in the Bitcoin network is about 10 minutes. With a 10-minute average time between blocks, 2016 blocks works out to two weeks. In other words, the recalculation of the target happens roughly every two weeks.

Let's think about what this means. If you're a miner, and you've invested a certain fixed amount of hardware into Bitcoin mining, but the overall mining ecosystem is growing, more miners are coming in, or they're deploying faster and faster hardware, that means that over a two week period, slightly more blocks are going to be found than expected. So nodes will automatically readjust the target, and the amount of work that you have to do to be able to find a block is going to increase. So if you put in a fixed amount of hardware investment, the rate at which you find blocks is actually dependent upon what other miners are doing. There's a very nice formula to capture this, which is that the probability that any given miner, Alice, is going to win the next block is equivalent to the fraction of global hash power that she controls. This means that if Alice has mining hardware that's about 0.1 percent of total hash power, she will find roughly one in every 1,000 blocks.

What is the purpose of this readjustment? Why do we want to maintain this 10-minute invariant? The reason is quite simple. If blocks were to come very close together, then there would be a lot of inefficiency, and we would lose the optimization benefits of being able to put a lot of transactions in a single block. There is nothing magical about the number 10, and if you went down from 10 minutes to 5 minutes, it would probably be just fine. There's been a lot of discussion about the ideal block latency that altcoins, or alternative cryptocurrencies, should have. But despite some disagreements about the ideal latency, everybody agrees that it should be a fixed amount. It cannot be allowed to go down without limit. That's why we have the automatic target recalculation feature.

The way that this cost function and proof of work is set up allows us to reformulate our security assumption. Here's where we finally depart from the last leap of faith that we asked you to take earlier. Instead of saying that somehow the majority of nodes are honest in a context where nodes don't even have identities and not being clear about what that means, we can now state crisply, that a lot of attacks on Bitcoin are infeasible if the majority of miners, weighted by hash power, are following the protocol — or, are honest. This is true because if a majority of miners, weighted by hash power, are honest, the competition for proposing the next block will automatically ensure that there is at least a 50 percent chance that the next block to be proposed at any point is coming from an honest node.

Sidebar. in the research fields of distributed systems and computer security, it is common to assume that some percentage of nodes are honest and to show that the system works as intended even if the other nodes behave arbitrarily. That's basically the approach we've taken here, except that we weight nodes by hash power in computing the majority. The original Bitcoin whitepaper contains this type of analysis as well.

But the field of game theory provides an entirely different, and arguably more sophisticated and realistic way to determine how a system will behave. In this view, we don't split nodes into honest and malicious. Instead, we assume that e *very* node acts according to its incentives. Each node picks a (randomized) strategy to maximize its payoff, taking into account other nodes' potential strategies. If the protocol and incentives are designed well, then most nodes will follow the rules most of the time. "Honest" behavior is just one strategy of many, and we attach no particular moral salience to it.

In the game theoretic view, the big question is whether the default miner behavior is a "Nash equilibrium," that is, whether it represents a stable situation in which no miner can realize a higher payoff by deviating from honest behavior. This question is still contentious and an active area of research.

Solving hash puzzles is probabilistic because nobody can predict which nonce is going to result in solving the hash puzzle. The only way to do it is to try nonces one by one and hope that one succeeds. Mathematically, this process is called **Bernoulli trials**. A Bernoulli trial is an experiment with two possible outcomes, and the probability of each outcome occurring is fixed between successive trials. Here, the two outcomes are whether or not the hash falls in the target, and assuming the hash functions behaves like a random function, the probability of those outcomes is fixed. Typically, nodes try so many nonces that Bernoulli trials, a discrete probability process, can be well approximated by a continuous probability process called a **Poisson process**, a process in which events occur independently at a constant average rate. The end result of all of that is that the probability density function that shows the relative likelihood of the time until the next block is found looks like Figure 2.5.

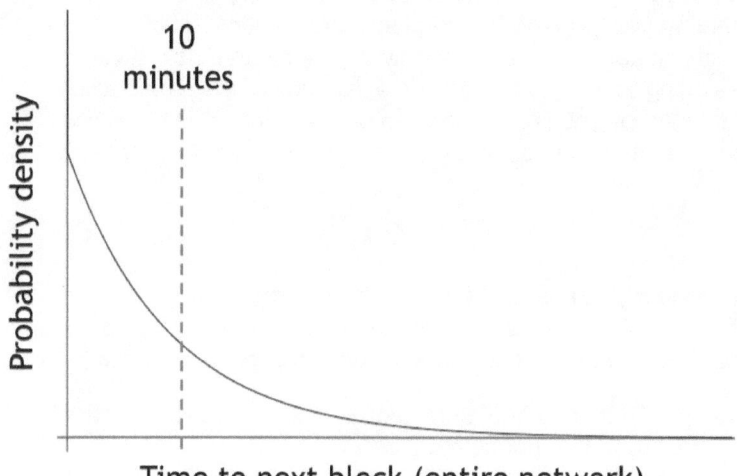

Figure 2.5 Probability density function of the time until the next block is found.

This is known as an exponential distribution. There is some small probability that if a block has been found now, the next block is going to be found very soon, say within a few seconds or a minute. And there is also some small probability that it will take a long time, say an hour, to find the next block. But overall, the network automatically adjusts the difficulty so that the inter-block time is maintained at an average, long term, of 10 minutes. Notice that Figure 2.5 shows how frequently blocks are going to be created by the entire network not caring about which miner actually finds the block.

If you're a miner, you're probably interested in how long it will take you to find a block. What does this probability density function look like? It's going to have the same shape, but it's just going to have a different scale on the x-axis. Again, it can be represented by a nice equation.For a specific miner:

mean time to next block = 10 minutes fraction of hash power

If you have 0.1 percent of the total network hash power, this equation tells us that you're going to find blocks once every 10,000 minutes, which is just about a week. Not only is your mean time between blocks going to be very high, but the variance of the time between blocks found by you is also going to be very high. This has some important consequences that we're going to look at in chapter 5.

Trivial to verify. L et's now turn to the third important property of this proof of work function, which is that it is trivial to verify that a node has computed proof of work correctly. Even if it takes a node, on

20 average, 10 tries to find a nonce that makes the block hash fall below the target, that nonce must be

published as part of the block. It is thus trivial for any other node to look at the block contents, hash them all together, and verify that the output is less than the target. This is quite an important property because, once again, it allows us to get rid of centralization. We don't need any centralized authority verifying that miners are doing their job correctly. Any node or any miner can instantly verify that a block found by another miner satisfies this proof-of-work property.

11.5 Putting it all together

Cost of mining. L et's now look at mining economics. We mentioned it's quite expensive to operate as 20

a miner. At the current difficulty level, finding a single block takes computing about 10 hashes and the block reward is about 25 Bitcoins, which is a sizable amount of money at the current exchange rate. These numbers allow for an easy calculation of whether it's profitable for one to mine, and we can capture this decision with a simple statement:

If **mining reward** > **m ining cost** then miner profits where

mining reward = block reward + tx feesm ining cost = hardware cost + operating costs (electricity, cooling, etc.)

Fundamentally, the mining reward that the miner gets is in terms of the block reward and transaction fees. The miner asks himself how it compares to the total expenditure, which is the hardware and electricity cost.

But there are some complications to this simple equation. The first is that, as you may have noticed, the hardware cost is a fixed cost whereas the electricity cost is a variable cost that is incurred over time. Another complication is that the reward that miners get depends upon the rate at which they find blocks, which depends on not just the power of their hardware, but on the ratio of their hash rate to the total global hash rate. A third complication is that the costs that the miner incurs are typically denominated in dollars or some other traditional currency, but their reward is denominated in bitcoin. So this equation has a hidden dependence on Bitcoin's exchange rate at any given time. And finally, so far we've assumed that the miner is interested in honestly following the protocol. But the miner might choose to use some other mining strategy instead of always attempting to extend the longest valid branch. So this equation doesn't capture all the nuances of the different strategies that the miner can employ. Actually analyzing whether it makes sense to mine is a complicated game theory problem that's not easily answered.

At this point, we've obtained a pretty good understanding of how a Bitcoin achieves decentralization. We will now recap the high level points and put it all together in order to get an even better understanding.

Let's start from identities. As we've learned, there are no real-world identities required to participate in the Bitcoin protocol. Any user can create a pseudonymous key pair at any moment, any number of them. When Alice wants to pay Bob in bitcoins, the Bitcoin protocol does not specify how Alice learns Bob's address. Given these pseudonymous key pairs as identities, transactions are basically messages that are broadcast to the Bitcoin peer-to-peer network that are instructions to transfer coins from one address to another. Bitcoins are just transaction outputs, and we will discuss this in much more detail in the next chapter.

The goal of the Bitcoin peer-to-peer network is to propagate all new transactions and new blocks to all the Bitcoin peer nodes. But the network is highly imperfect, and does a best-effort attempt to relay this information. The security of the system doesn't come from the perfection of the peer-to-peer network. Instead, the security comes from the block chain and the consensus protocol that we devoted much of this chapter to studying.

When we say that a transaction is included in the block chain, what we really mean is that the transaction has achieved numerous confirmations. There's no fixed number to how many confirmations are necessary before we are sufficiently convinced of its inclusion, but six is a commonly-used heuristic. The more confirmations a transaction has received, the more certain you can be that this transaction is part of the consensus chain. There will often be orphan blocks, or blocks that don't make it into the consensus chain. There are a variety of reasons that could lead to a block being orphaned. The block may contain an invalid transaction, or a double-spend attempt. It could also just be a result of network latency. That is, two miners may simply end up finding new blocks within just a few seconds of each other. So both of these blocks were broadcast nearly simultaneously onto the network, and one of them will inevitably be orphaned.

Finally, we looked at hash puzzles and mining. Miners are special types of nodes that decide to compete in this game of creating new blocks. They're rewarded for their effort in terms of both newly minted bitcoins (the new-block reward) and existing bitcoins (transaction fees), provided that other miners build upon their blocks. A subtle but crucial point: say that Alice and Bob are two different miners, and Alice has 100 times as much computing power as Bob. This does not mean that Alice will always win the race against Bob to find the next block. Instead, Alice and Bob have a probability ratio

Sidebar. Bitcoin doesn't have fixed denominations like US dollars, and in particular, there is no special designation of "1 bitcoin."

Bitcoins are just transaction outputs, and in the current rules, they can have an arbitrary value with 8 decimal places of precision. The smallest possible value is 0.00000001 B T C (bitcoins), which is called 1 **Satoshi**.

of finding the next block, in the proportion 100 to 1. In the long term, Bob will find, on average, one percent of the number of blocks that Alice finds.

We expect that miners will typically be somewhere close to the economic equilibrium in the sense that the expenditure that they incur in terms of hardware and electricity will be roughly equal to the rewards that they obtain. The reason is that if a miner is consistently making a loss, she will probably stop mining. On the other hand, and if mining is very profitable given typical hardware and electricity costs, then more mining hardware would enter the network. The increased hash rate would lead to an increase in the difficulty, and each miner's expected reward would drop.

This notion of distributed consensus permeates Bitcoin quite deeply. In a traditional currency, consensus does come into play to a certain limited extent. Specifically, there is a consensus process that determines the exchange rate of the currency. That is certainly true in Bitcoin as well; We need consensus around the value of Bitcoin. But in Bitcoin, additionally, we need consensus on the state of the ledger, which is what the block chain accomplishes. In other words, even the accounting of how many bitcoins you own is subject to consensus. When we say that Alice owns a certain amount or number of bitcoins, what we actually mean is that the Bitcoin peer-to-peer network, as recorded in the block chain, considers the sum total of all Alice's addresses to own that number of bitcoins. That is ultimate nature of truth in Bitcoin: ownership of bitcoins is nothing more than other nodes agreeing that a given party owns those bitcoins.

Finally, we need consensus about the rules of the system because occasionally, the rules of the system have to change. There are two types of changes to the rules of Bitcoin, known respectively as **soft forks** and **hardforks**. We are going to defer this discussion of the differences to later chapters in which we will discuss them in detail.

Getting a cryptocurrency off the ground. A nother subtle concept is that of ***b ootstrapping***. There is a tricky interplay between three different ideas in Bitcoin: the security of the block chain, the health of the mining ecosystem, and the value of the currency. We obviously want the block chain to be secure for Bitcoin to be a viable currency. For the block chain to be secure, an adversary must not be able to overwhelm the consensus process. This in turn means that an adversary cannot create a lot of mining nodes and take over 50 percent or more of the new block creation.

But when will that be true? A prerequisite is having a healthy mining ecosystem made up of largely honest, protocol-following nodes. But what's a prerequisite for that — when can we be sure that a lot of miners will put a lot of computing power into participating in this hash puzzle solving competition? Well, they're only going to do that if the exchange rate of Bitcoin is pretty high because the rewards that they receive are denominated in Bitcoins whereas their expenditure is in dollars. So the more the value of the currency goes up, the more incentivized these miners are going to be.

But what ensures a high and stable value of the currency? That can only happen if users in general have trust in the security of the block chain. If they believe that the network could be overwhelmed at any moment by an attacker, then Bitcoin is not going to have a lot of value as a currency. So you have this interlocking interdependence between the security of the block chain, a healthy mining ecosystem and the exchange rate.

Because of the cyclical nature of this three-way dependence, the existence of each of these is predicated on the existence of the others. When Bitcoin was first created, none of these three existed. There were no miners other than Nakamoto himself running the mining software. Bitcoin didn't have a lot of value as a currency. And the block chain was, in fact, insecure because there was not a lot of mining going on and anybody could have easily overwhelmed this process.

There's no simple explanation for how Bitcoin went from not having any of these properties to having all three of them. Media attention was part of the story — the more people hear about Bitcoin, the more they're going to get interested in mining. And the more they get interested in mining, the more confidence people will have in the security of the block chain because there's now more mining activity going on, and so forth. Incidentally, every new Altcoin that wants to succeed also has to somehow solve this problem of pulling itself up by its bootstraps.

51-percent attack. F inally, let's consider what would happen if consensus failed and there was in fact a *5 1-percent attacker* who controls 51 percent or more of the mining power in the Bitcoin network. We'll consider a variety of possible attacks and see which ones can actually be carried out by such an attacker.

First of all, can this attacker steal coins from an existing address? As you may have guessed, the answer is no, because stealing from an existing address is not possible unless you subvert the cryptography. It's not enough to subvert the consensus process. This is not completely obvious. Let's say the 51 percent attacker creates an invalid block that contains an invalid transaction that represents stealing Bitcoins from an existing address that the attacker doesn't control and transferring them to his own address. The attacker can pretend that it's a valid transaction and keep building upon this block. The attacker can even succeed in making that the longest branch. But the other honest nodes are simply not going to accept this block with an invalid transaction and are going to keep mining based on the last valid block that they found in the network. So what will happen is that there will be what we call a fork in the chain.

Now imagine this from the point of view of the attacker trying to spend these invalid coins, and send them to some merchant Bob as payment for some goods or service. Bob is presumably running a Bitcoin node himself, and it will be an honest node. Bob's node will reject that branch as invalid because it contains an invalid transaction. It's invalid because the signatures didn't check out. So Bob's node will simply ignore the longest branch because it's an invalid branch. And because of that, subverting consensus is not enough. You have to subvert cryptography to steal bitcoins. So we conclude that this attack is not possible for a 51 percent attacker.

We should note that all this is only a thought experiment. If there were, in fact, actual signs of a 51 percent attack, what will probably happen is that the developers will notice this and react to it. They will update the Bitcoin software, and we might expect that the rules of the system, including the peer-to-peer network, might change in some form to make it more difficult for this attack to succeed. But we can't quite predict that. So we're working in a simplified model where a 51 percent attack happens, but other than that, there are no changes or tweaks to the rules of the system.

Let's consider another attack. Can the 51-percent attacker suppress some transactions? Let's say there is some user, Carol, whom the attacker really doesn't like. The attacker knows some of Carol's addresses, and wants to make sure that no coins belonging to any of those addresses can possibly be spent. Is that possible? Since he controls the consensus process of the block chain, the attacker can simply refuse to create any new blocks that contain transactions from one of Carol's addresses. The attacker can further refuse to build upon blocks that contain such transactions. However, he can't prevent these transactions from being broadcast to the peer-to-peer network because the network doesn't depend on the block chain, or on consensus, and we're assuming that the attacker doesn't fully control the network. The attacker cannot stop the transactions from reaching the majority of nodes, so even if the attack succeeds, it will at least be apparent that the attack is happening.

Can the attacker change the block reward? That is, can the attacker start pretending that the block reward is, instead of 25 Bitcoins, say 100 Bitcoins? This is a change to the rules of the system, and because the attacker doesn't control the copies of the Bitcoin software that all of the honest nodes are running, this is also not possible. This is similar to the reason why the attacker cannot include invalid transactions. Other nodes will simply not recognize the increase in the block reward, and the attacker will thus be unable to spend them.

Finally, can the attacker somehow destroy confidence in Bitcoin? Well, let's imagine what would happen. If there were a variety of double-spend attempts, situations in which nodes did not extend the longest valid branch, and other attempted attacks, then people are going to likely decide that Bitcoin is no longer acting as a decentralized ledger that they can trust. People will lose confidence in the currency, and we might expect that the exchange rate of Bitcoin will plummet. In fact, if it is known that there is a party that controls 51 percent of the hash power, then it's possible that people will lose confidence in Bitcoin even if the attacker is not necessarily trying to launch any attacks. So it is not only possible, but in fact likely, that a 51 percent attacker of any sort will destroy confidence in the currency. Indeed, this is the main practical threat if a 51 percent attack were ever to materialize. Considering the amount of expenditure that the adversary would have to put into attacking Bitcoin and achieving a 51 percent majority, none of the other attacks that we described really make sense from a financial point of view.

Hopefully, at this point you've obtained a really good understanding of how decentralization is achieved in Bitcoin. You should have a good command on how identities work in Bitcoin, how transactions are propagated and validated, the role of the peer-to-peer network in Bitcoin, how the block chain is used to achieve consensus, and how hash puzzles and mining work. These concepts provide a solid foundation and a good launching point for understanding a lot of the more subtle details and nuances of Bitcoin, which we're going to see in the coming chapters.

1. Why do miners run "full nodes" that keep track of the entire block chain[2] whereas Bob the merchant can get away with a "lite node" that implements "simplified payment verification," needing to examine only the last few blocks?

2. If a malicious ISP completely controls a user's connections, can it launch a double-spend attack against the user? How much computational effort would this take?

3. Consider Bob the merchant deciding whether or not to accept the C $_A \rightarrow$ B transaction. What Bob is really interested in is whether or not the other chain will catch up. Why, then, does he simply check how many confirmations C $_A \rightarrow$ B has received, instead of computing the difference in length between the two chains?

[2] This only applies to "solo" miners who're not part of a mining pool, but we haven't discussed that yet.

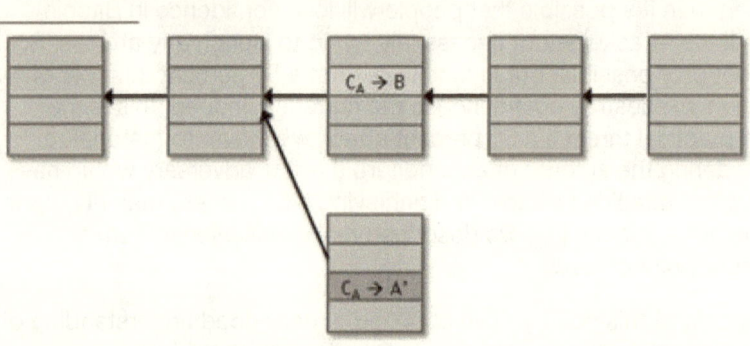

4. Even when all nodes are honest, blocks will occasionally get orphaned: if two miners Minnie and Mynie discover blocks nearly simultaneously, neither will have time to hear about the other's block before broadcasting hers.

4a. What determines whose block will end up on the consensus branch?

4b. What factors affect the rate of orphan blocks? Can you derive a formula for the rate based on these parameters?

4c. Try to empirically measure this rate on the Bitcoin network.

4d. If Mynie hears about Minnie's block just before she's about to discover hers, does that mean she wasted her effort?

4e. Do all miners have their blocks orphaned at the same rate, or are some miners affected disproportionately?

5a. How can a miner establish an identity in a way that's hard to fake? (i.e., anyone can tell which blocks were mined by her.)

5b. If a miner misbehaves, can other miners "boycott" her by refusing to build on her blocks on an ongoing basis?

6a. Assuming that the total hash power of the network stays constant, what is the probability that a block will be found in the next 10 minutes?

6b. Suppose Bob the merchant wants to have a policy that orders will ship within x minutes after receipt of payment. What value of x should Bob choose so that with 99% confidence 6 blocks will be found within x minutes?

12 MECHANICS OF BITCOIN

This chapter is about the mechanics of Bitcoin. Whereas in the first two chapters, we've talked at a relatively high level, now we're going to delve into detail. We'll look at real data structures, real scripts, and try to learn the details and language of Bitcoin in a precise way to set up everything that we want to talk about in the rest of this book. This chapter will be challenging because a lot of details will be flying at you. You'll learn the specifics and the quirks that make Bitcoin what it is.

To recap where we left off last time, the Bitcoin consensus mechanism gives us an append-only ledger, a data structure that we can only write to. Once data is written to it, it's there forever. There's a decentralized protocol for establishing consensus about the value of that ledger, and there are miners who perform that protocol and validate transactions. Together they make sure that transactions are well formed, that they aren't already spent, and that the ledger and network can function as a currency. At the same time, we assumed that a currency existed to motivate these miners. In this chapter we'll look at the details of how we actually build that currency, to motivate the miners that make this whole process happen.

12.1 Bitcoin transactions

Let's start with transactions, Bitcoin's fundamental building block. We're going to use a simplified model of a ledger for the moment. Instead of blocks, let's suppose individual transactions are added to the ledger one at a time.

Figure 3.1 an account-based ledger

How can we build a currency on top of such a ledger? The first model you might think of, which is actually the mental model many people have for how Bitcoin works, is that you have an account-based system. You can add some transactions that create new coins and credit them to somebody. And then later you can transfer them. A transaction would say something like "we're moving 17 coins from Alice to Bob", and it will be signed by Alice. That's all the information about the

Create 25 coins and credit to Alice_{ASSERTED BY MINERS}
Transfer 17 coins from Alice to Bob_{SIGNED(Alice)}
Transfer 8 coins from Bob to Carol_{SIGNED(Bob)}
Transfer 5 coins from Carol to Alice_{SIGNED(Carol)}
Transfer 15 coins from Alice to David_{SIGNED(Alice)}

transaction that's contained in the ledger. In Figure 3.1, after Alice receives 25 coins in the first transaction and then transfers 17 coins to Bob in the second, she'd have 8 Bitcoins left in her account.

The downside to this way of doing things is that anyone who wants to determine if a transaction is valid will have to keep track of these account balances. Take another look at Figure 3.1. Does Alice have the 15 coins that she's trying to transfer to David? To figure this out, you'd have to look backwards in time forever to see every transaction affecting Alice, and whether or not her net balance at the time that she tries to transfer 15 coins to David is greater than 15 coins. Of course we can make this a little bit more efficient with some data structures that track Alice's balance after each transaction. But that's going to require a lot of extra housekeeping besides the ledger itself.

Because of these downsides, Bitcoin doesn't use an account-based model. Instead, Bitcoin uses a ledger that just keeps track of transactions similar to ScroogeCoin in Chapter 1.

Figure 3.2 a transaction-based ledger, which is very close to Bitcoin

Transactions specify a number of inputs and a number of outputs (recall PayCoins in ScroogeCoin). You can think of the inputs as coins being consumed (created in a previous transaction) and the outputs as coins being created. For transactions in which new currency is being minted, there are no coins being consumed (recall CreateCoins in ScroogeCoin). Each transaction has a unique identifier. Outputs are indexed beginning with 0, so we will refer to the first output as "output 0".

Let's now work our way through Figure 3.2. Transaction 1 has no inputs because this transaction is creating new coins, and it has an output of 25 coins going to Alice. Also, since this is a transaction where new coins are being created, no signature is required. Now let's say that Alice wants to send some of those coins over to Bob. To do so, she creates a new transaction, transaction 2 in our example. In the transaction, she has to explicitly refer to the previous transaction where these coins are coming from. Here, she refers to output 0 of transaction 1 (indeed the only output of transaction 1), which assigned 25 bitcoins to Alice. She also must specify the output addresses in the transaction.

1	Inputs: Ø Outputs: 25.0→Alice
2	Inputs: 1[0] Outputs: 17.0→Bob, 8.0→Alice <div align="right">SIGNED(Alice)</div>
3	Inputs: 2[0] Outputs: 8.0→Carol, 9.0→Bob <div align="right">SIGNED(Bob)</div>
4	Inputs: 2[1] Outputs: 6.0→David, 2.0→Alice <div align="right">SIGNED(Alice)</div>

76

In this example, Alice specifies two outputs, 17 coins to Bob, and 8 coins to Alice. And, of course, this whole thing is signed by Alice, so that we know that Alice actually authorizes this transaction.

Change addresses. W hy does Alice have to send money to herself in this example? Just as coins in ScroogeCoin are immutable, in Bitcoin, the entirety of a transaction output must be consumed by another transaction, or none of it. Alice only wants to pay 17 bitcoins to Bob, but the output that she owns is worth 25 bitcoins. So she needs to create a new output where 8 bitcoins are sent back to herself. It could be a different address from the one that owned the 25 bitcoins, but it would have to be owned by her. This is called a ***c hange address***.

Efficient verification. W hen a new transaction is added to the ledger, how easy is it to check if it is valid? In this example, we need to look up the transaction output that Alice referenced, make sure that it has a value of 25 bitcoins, and that it hasn't already been spent. Looking up the transaction output is easy since we're using hash pointers. To ensure it hasn't been spent, we need to scan the block chain between the referenced transaction and the latest block. We don't need to go all the way back to the beginning of the block chain, and it doesn't require keeping any additional data structures (although, as we'll see, additional data structures will speed things up).

Consolidating funds. A s in ScroogeCoin, since transactions can have many inputs and many outputs, splitting and merging value is easy. For example, say Bob received money in two different transactions — 17 bitcoins in one, and 2 in another. Bob might say, I'd like to have one transaction I can spend later where I have all 19 bitcoins. That's easy — he creates a transaction with the two inputs and one output, with the output address being one that he owns. That lets him consolidate those two transactions.

Joint payments. S imilarly, joint payments are also easy to do. Say Carol and Bob both want to pay David. They can create a transaction with two inputs and one output, but with the two inputs owned by two different people. And the only difference from the previous example is that since the two outputs from prior transactions that are being claimed here are from different addresses, the transaction will need two separate signatures — one by Carol and one by Bob.

Transaction syntax. C onceptually that's really all there is to a Bitcoin transaction. Now let's see how it's represented at a low level in Bitcoin. Ultimately, every data structure that's sent on the network is a string of bits. What's shown in Figure 3.3 is very low-level, but this further gets compiled down to a compact binary format that's not human-readable.

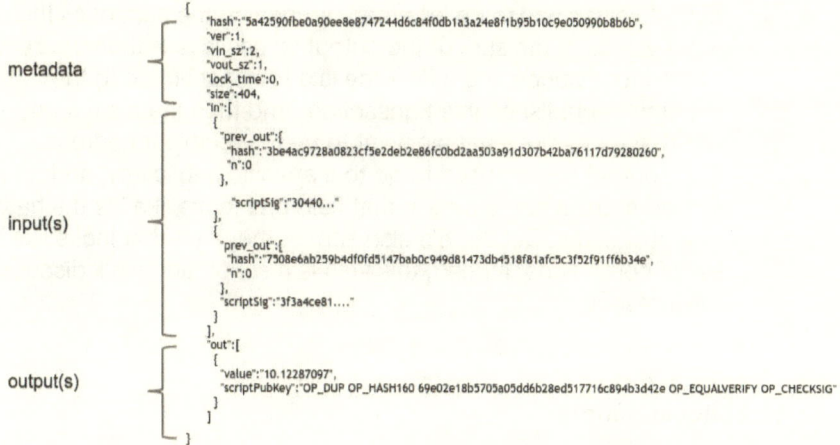

```
{
  "hash":"5a42590fbe0a90ee8e8747244d6c84f0db1a3a24e8f1b95b10c9e050990b8b6b",
  "ver":1,
  "vin_sz":2,
  "vout_sz":1,
  "lock_time":0,
  "size":404,
  "in":[
    {
      "prev_out":{
        "hash":"3be4ac9728a0823cf5e2deb2e86fc0bd2aa503a91d307b42ba76117d79280260",
        "n":0
      },
      "scriptSig":"30440..."
    },
    {
      "prev_out":{
        "hash":"7508e6ab259b4df0fd5147bab0c949d81473db4518f81afc5c3f52f91ff6b34e",
        "n":0
      },
      "scriptSig":"3f3a4ce81...."
    }
  ],
  "out":[
    {
      "value":"10.12287097",
      "scriptPubKey":"OP_DUP OP_HASH160 69e02e18b5705a05dd6b28ed517716c894b3d42e OP_EQUALVERIFY OP_CHECKSIG"
    }
  ]
}
```

metadata · input(s) · output(s)

***Figure 3.3** An actual Bitcoin transaction.*

As you can see in Figure 3.3, there are three parts to a transaction: some metadata, a series of inputs, and a series of outputs.

- **Metadata**. There's some housekeeping information — the size of the transaction, the number of inputs, and the number of outputs. There's the hash of the entire transaction which serves as a unique ID for the transaction. That's what allows us to use hash pointers to reference transactions. Finally there's a "lock_time" field, which we'll come back to later.

- **Inputs.** The transaction inputs form an array, and each input has the same form. An input specifies a previous transaction, so it contains a hash of that transaction, which acts as a hash pointer to it. The input also contains the index of the previous transaction's outputs that's being claimed. And then there's a signature. Remember that we have to sign to show that we actually have the ability to claim those previous transaction outputs.

- **Outputs.** The outputs are again an array. Each output has just two fields. They each have a value, and the sum of all the output values has to be less than or equal to the sum of all the input values. If the sum of the output values is less than the sum of the input values, the difference is a transaction fee to the miner who publishes this transaction. And then there's a funny line that looks like what we want to be the recipient address. Each output is supposed to go to a specific public key, and indeed there is something in that field that looks like it's the hash of a public key. But there's also some other stuff that looks like a set of commands. Indeed, this field is a script, and we'll discuss this presently.

12.2 Bitcoin Scripts

Each transaction output doesn't just specify a public key. It actually specifies a script. What is a script, and why do we use scripts? In this section we'll study the Bitcoin scripting language and understand why a script is used instead of simply assigning a public key.

The most common type of transaction in Bitcoin is to redeem a previous transaction output by signing with the correct key. In this case, we want the transaction output to say, "this can be redeemed by a signature from the owner of address X." Recall that an address is a hash of a public key. So merely specifying the address X doesn't tell us what the public key is, and doesn't give us a way to check the signature ! So instead the transaction output must say : "this can be redeemed by a public key that hashes to X, along with a signature from the owner of that public key." As we'll see, this is exactly what the most common type of script in Bitcoin says.

OP_DUP OP_HASH160 69e02e18... OP_EQUALVERIFY OP_CHECKSIG

Figure 3.4. an example Pay-to-PubkeyHash script, the most common type of output script in Bitcoin

But what happens to this script? Who runs it, and how exactly does this sequence of instructions enforce the above statement? The secret is that the inputs also contain scripts instead of signatures. To validate that a transaction redeems a previous transaction output correctly, we combine the new transaction's input script and the earlier transaction's output script. We simply concatenate them, and the resulting script must run successfully in order for the transaction to be valid. These two scripts are called *s criptPubKey* and *s criptSig* because in the simplest case, the output script just specifies a public key (or an address to which the public key hashes), and the input script specifies a signature with that public key. The combined script can be seen in Figure 3.5.

Bitcoin scripting language. T he scripting language was built specifically for Bitcoin, and is just called 'Script' or the Bitcoin scripting language. It has many similarities to a language called Forth, which is an old, simple, stack-based, programming language. But you don't need to understand Forth to understand Bitcoin scripting. The key design goals for Script were to have something simple and compact, yet with native support for cryptographic operations. So, for example, there are special-purpose instructions to compute hash functions and to compute and verify signatures.

The scripting language is stack-based. This means that every instruction is executed exactly once, in a linear manner. In particular, there are no loops in the Bitcoin scripting language. So the number of instructions in the script gives us an upper bound on how long it might take to run and how much memory it could use. The language is not Turing-complete, which means that it doesn't have the ability to compute arbitrarily powerful functions. And this is by design — miners have to run these scripts, which are submitted by arbitrary participants in the network. We don't want to give them the power to submit a script that might have an infinite loop.

<sig> <pubKey> -------------- OP_DUP OP_HASH160 <pubKeyHash?> OP_EQUALVERIFY OP_CHECKSIG

Figure 3.5. To check if a transaction correctly redeems an output, we create a combined script by appending the scriptPubKey of the referenced output transaction (bottom) to the scriptSig of the redeeming transaction (top). Notice that <pubKeyHash?> contains a

'?'. We use this notation to indicate that we will later check to confirm that this is equal to the hash of the public key provided in the redeeming script.

There are only two possible outcomes when a Bitcoin script is executed. It either executes successfully with no errors, in which case the transaction is valid. Or, if there's any error while the script is executing, the whole transaction will be invalid and shouldn't be accepted into the block chain.

The Bitcoin scripting language is very small. There's only room for 256 instructions, because each one is represented by one byte. Of those 256, 15 are currently disabled, and 75 are reserved. The reserved instruction codes haven't been assigned any specific meaning yet, but might be instructions that are added later in time.

Many of the basic instructions are those you'd expect to be in any programming language. There's basic arithmetic, basic logic — like 'if' and 'then' — , throwing errors, not throwing errors, and returning early. Finally, there are crypto instructions which include hash functions, instructions for signature verification, as well as a special and important instruction called CHECKMULTISIG that lets you check multiple signatures with one instruction. Figure 3.6 lists some of the most common instructions in the Bitcoin scripting language.

The CHECKMULTISIG instruction requires specifying *n* public keys, and a parameter *t* , for a threshold. For this instruction to execute validly, there have to be at least *t* signatures from *t* out of *n* of those public keys that are valid. We'll show some examples of what you'd use multisignatures for in the next section, but it should be immediately clear this is quite a powerful primitive. We can express in a compact way the concept that *t* out of *n* specified entities must sign in order for the transaction to be valid.

Incidentally, there's a bug in the multisignature implementation, and it's been there all along. The CHECKMULTISIG instruction pops an extra data value off the stack and ignores it. This is just a quirk of

the Bitcoin language and one has to deal with it by putting an extra dummy variable onto the stack. The bug was in the original implementation, and the costs of fixing it are much higher than the damage it causes, as we'll see later in Section 3.5. At this point, this bug is considered a feature in Bitcoin, in that it's not going away.

OP_DUP	Duplicates the top item on the stack
OP_HASH160	Hashes twice: first using SHA-256 and then RIPEMD-160
OP_EQUALVERIFY	Returns true if the inputs are equal. Returns false and marks the transaction as invalid if they are unequal
OP_CHECKSIG	Checks that the input signature is a valid signature using the input public key for the hash of the current transaction
OP_CHECKMULTISIG	Checks that the k signatures on the transaction are valid signatures from k of the specified public keys.

Figure 3.6 a list of common Script instructions and their functionality.

Executing a script. T o execute a script in a stack-based programming language, all we'll need is a stack that we can push data to and pop data from. We won't need any other memory or variables. That's what makes it so computationally simple. There are two types of instructions: data instructions and opcodes. When a data instruction appears in a script, that data is simply pushed onto the top of the stack. Opcodes, on the other hand, perform some function, often taking as input data that is on top of the stack.

Now let's look at how the Bitcoin script in Figure 3.5 is executed. Refer to Figure 3.7, where we show the state of the stack after each instruction. The first two instructions in this script are data instructions — the signature and the public key used to verify that signature — specified in the scriptSig component of a transaction input in the redeeming transaction. As we mentioned, when we see a data instruction, we just push it onto the stack. The rest of the script was specified in the scriptPubKey component of a transaction output in the referenced transaction.

First we have the duplicate instruction, OP_DUP, so we just push a copy of the public key onto the top of the stack. The next instruction is OP_HASH160, which tells us to pop the top value, compute its cryptographic hash, and push the result onto the top of the stack. When this instruction finishes executing, we will have replaced the public key on the top of the stack with its hash.

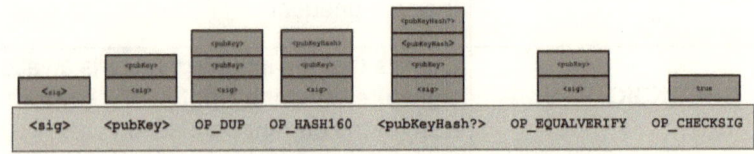

Figure 3.7 **Execution of a Bitcoin script.** O n the bottom, we show the instruction in the script. Data instructions are denoted with surrounding angle brackets, whereas opcodes begin with "OP_". On the top, we show the stack just after that instruction has been executed.

Next, we're going to do one more push of data onto the stack. Recall that this data was specified by the sender of the referenced transaction. It is the hash of a public key that the sender specified; the corresponding private key must be used to generate the signature to redeem these coins. At this point, there are two values at the top of the stack. There is the hash of the public key, as specified by the sender, and the hash of the public key that was used by the recipient when trying to claim the coins.

At this point we'll run the EQUALVERIFY command, which checks that the two values at the top of the stack are equal. If they aren't, an error will be thrown, and the script will stop executing. But in our example, we'll assume that they're equal, that is, that the recipient of the coins used the correct public key. That instruction will consume those two data items that are at the top of the stack, And the stack now contains two items — a signature and the public key.

We've already checked that this public key is in fact the public key that the referenced transaction specified, and now we have to check if the signature is valid. This is a great example of where the Bitcoin scripting language is built with cryptography in mind. Even though it's a fairly simple language in terms of logic, there are some quite powerful instructions in there, like this "OP_CHECKSIG" instruction. This single instruction pops those two values off of the stack, and does the entire signature verification in one go.

But what is this a signature of? What is the input to the signature function? It turns out there's only one thing you can sign in Bitcoin — an entire transaction. So the "CHECKSIG" instruction pops the two values, the public key and signature, off the stack, and verifies that is a valid signature for the entire transaction using that public key. Now we've executed every instruction in the script, and there's nothing left on the stack. Provided there weren't any errors, the output of this script will simply be **true** indicating that the transaction is valid.

What's used in practice. I n theory, Script lets us specify, in some sense, arbitrary conditions that must be met in order to spend coins. But, as of today, this flexibility isn't used very heavily. If we look at the scripts that have actually been used in the history of Bitcoin so far, the vast majority, 99.9 percent, are exactly the same script, which is in fact the script that we used in our example. As we saw, this script just specifies one public key and requires a signature for that public key in order to spend the coins. There are a few other instructions that do get some use. MULTISIG gets used a little bit as does a special type of script called Pay-to-Script-Hash which we'll discuss shortly. But other than that, there hasn't been much diversity in terms of what scripts get used. This is because Bitcoin nodes, by default, have a whitelist of standard scripts, and they refuse to accept scripts that are not on the list. This doesn't mean that those scripts can't be used at all; it just makes them harder to use. In fact this distinction is a very subtle point which we'll return to in a bit when we talk about the Bitcoin peer-to-peer network.

Proof of burn. A proof-of-burn is a script that can never be redeemed. Sending coins to a proof-of-burn script establishes that they have been destroyed since there's no possible way for them to be spent. One use of proof-of-burn is to bootstrap an alternative to Bitcoin by forcing people to destroy Bitcoin in order to gain coins in the new system. We'll discuss this in more detail in Chapter 10. Proof-of-burn is quite simple to implement: the OP_RETURN opcode throws an error if it's ever reached. No matter what values you put before OP_RETURN, that instruction will get executed eventually, in which case this script will return false.

Because the error is thrown, the data in the script that comes after OP_RETURN will not be processed. So this is an opportunity for people to put arbitrary data in a script, and hence into the block chain. If, for some reason, you want to write your name, or if you want to timestamp and prove that you knew some data at a specific time, you can create a very low value Bitcoin transaction. You can destroy a very small amount of currency, but you get to write whatever you want into the block chain, which should be kept around forever.

Pay-to-script-hash. O ne consequence of the way that Bitcoin scripts works is that the sender of coins has to specify the script exactly. But this can sometimes be quite a strange way of doing things. Say, for example, you're a consumer shopping online, and you're about to order something. And you say, "Alright, I'm ready to pay. Tell me the address to which I should send my coins." Now, say that the company that you're ordering from is using MULTISIG addresses. Then, since the one spending the coins has to specify this, the retailer will have to come back and say, "Oh, well, we're doing something fancy now. We're using MULTISIG. We're going to ask you to send the coins to some complicated script." You might say, "I don't know how to do that. That's too complicated. As a consumer, I just want to send to a simple address."

Bitcoin has a clever solution to this problem, and it applies to not just multi-sig addresses but to any complicated condition governing when coins can be spent. Instead of telling the sender "send your coins to the hash of this public key", the receiver can instead tell the sender "send your coins to the hash of this s cript. Impose the condition that to redeem those coins, it is necessary to reveal the script that has the given hash, and further, provide data that will make the script evaluate to true." The sender achieves this by using the Pay-to-script-hash (P2SH) transaction type, which has the above semantics.

Specifically, the P2SH script simply hashes the top value on the stack, checks if it matches the provided hash value, then executes a special second step of validation: that top data value from the stack is reinterpreted as a sequence of instructions, and executed a second time as a script, with the rest of the stack as input.

Getting support for P2SH was quite complicated since it wasn't part of Bitcoin's initial design specification. It was added after the fact. This is probably the most notable feature that's been added to Bitcoin that wasn't there in the original specification. And it solves a couple of important problems. It removes complexity from the sender, so the recipient can just specify a hash that the sender sends money to. In our example above, Alice need not worry that Bob is using multisig; she just sends to Bob's P2SH address, and it is Bob's responsibility to specify the fancy script when he wants to redeem the coins.

P2SH also has a nice efficiency gain. Miners have to track the set of output scripts that haven't been redeemed yet, and with P2SH outputs, the output scripts are now much smaller as they only specify a hash. All of the complexity is pushed to the input scripts.

12.3 Applications of Bitcoin scripts

Now that we understand how Bitcoin scripts work, let's take a look at some of the powerful applications that can be realized with this scripting language. It turns out we can do many neat things that will justify the complexity of having the scripting language instead of just specifying public keys.

Escrow transactions. S ay Alice and Bob want to do business with each other — Alice wants to pay Bob in Bitcoin for Bob to send some physical goods to Alice. The problem though is that Alice doesn't want to pay until after she's received the goods, but Bob doesn't want to send the goods until after he has been paid. What can we do about that? A nice solution in Bitcoin that's been used in practice is to introduce a third party and do an escrow transaction.

Escrow transactions can be implemented quite simply using MULTISIG. Alice doesn't send the money directly to Bob, but instead creates a MULTISIG transaction that requires two of three people to sign in order to redeem the coins. And those three people are going to be Alice, Bob, and some third party arbitrator, Judy, who will come into play in case there's any dispute. So Alice creates a 2-of-3 MULTISIG transaction that sends some coins she owns and specifies that they can be spent if any two of Alice, Bob, and Judy sign. This transaction is included in the block chain, and at this point, these coins are held in escrow between Alice, Bob, and Judy, such that any two of them can specify where the coins should go. At this point, Bob is convinced that it's safe to send the goods over to Alice, so he'll mail them or deliver them physically. Now in the normal case, Alice and Bob are both honest. So, Bob will send over the goods that Alice is expecting, and when Alice receives the goods, Alice and Bob both sign a transaction redeeming the funds from escrow, and sending them to Bob. Notice that in this case where both Alice and Bob are honest, Judy never had to get involved at all. There was no dispute, and Alice's and Bob's signatures met the 2-of-3 requirement of the MULTISIG transaction. So in the normal case, this isn't that much less efficient than Alice just sending Bob the money. It requires just one extra transaction on the block chain.

But what would have happened if Bob didn't actually send the goods or they got lost in the mail? Or perhaps the goods were different than what Alice ordered? Alice now doesn't want to pay Bob because she thinks that she got cheated, and she wants to get her money back. So Alice is definitely not going to sign a transaction that releases the money to Bob. But Bob also may deny any wrongdoing and refuse to sign a transaction that releases the money back to Alice. This is where Judy needs to get involved. Judy's going to have to decide which of these two people deserves the money. If Judy decides that Bob cheated, Judy will be willing to sign a transaction along with Alice, sending the money from escrow back to Alice. Alice's and Judy's signatures meet the 2-of-3 requirement of the MULTISIG transaction, and Alice will get her money back. And, of course, if Judy thinks that Alice is at fault here, and Alice is simply refusing to pay when she should, Judy can sign a transaction along with Bob, sending the money to Bob. So Judy decides between the two possible outcomes. But the nice thing is that she won't have to be involved unless there's a dispute.

Green addresses. Another cool application is what are called green addresses. Say Alice wants to pay Bob, and Bob's offline. Since he's offline, Bob can't go and look at the block chain to see if a transaction that Alice is sending is actually there. It's also possible that Bob is online, but doesn't have the time to go and look at the block chain and wait for the transactions to be confirmed. Remember that normally we want a transaction to be in the block chain and be confirmed by six blocks, which takes up to an hour, before we trust that it's really in the block chain. But for some merchandise such as food, Bob can't wait an hour before delivering. If Bob were a street vendor selling hot dogs, it's unlikely that Alice would wait around for an hour to receive her food. Or maybe Bob for some other reason doesn't have any connection to the Internet at all, and is thus not going to be able to check the block chain.

To solve this problem of being able to send money using Bitcoin without the recipient being able to access the block chain, we have to introduce another third party, which we'll call the bank (in practice it could be an exchange or any other financial intermediary). Alice is going to talk to her bank, and say, "Hey, it's me, Alice. I'm your loyal customer. Here's my card or my identification. And I'd really like to pay Bob here, could you help me out?" And the bank will say, "Sure. I'm going to deduct some money out of your account. And draw up a transaction from one of my green addresses over to Bob."

So notice that this money is coming directly from the bank to Bob. Some of the money, of course, might be in a change address going back to the bank. But essentially, the bank is paying Bob here from a bank-controlled address, which we call a green address. Moreover, the bank guarantees that it will not double-spend this money. So as soon as Bob sees that this transaction is signed by the bank, if he trusts the bank's guarantee not to double-spend the money, he can accept that that money will eventually be his when it's confirmed in the block chain.

Notice that this is not a Bitcoin-enforced guarantee. This is a real-world guarantee, and in order for this system to work, Bob has to trust that the bank, in the real world, cares about their reputation, and won't double-spend for that reason. And the bank will be able to say, "You can look at my history. I've been using this green address for a long time, and I've never double spent. Therefore I'm very unlikely to do so in the future." Thus Bob no longer has to trust Alice, whom he may know nothing about. Instead, he places his trust in the bank that they will not double-spend the money that they sent him.

Of course, if the bank ever does double-spend, people will stop trusting its green address(es). In fact, the two most prominent online services that implemented green addresses were Instawallet and Mt. Gox, and both ended up collapsing. Today green addresses aren't used very much. When the idea was first proposed, it generated much excitement as a way to do payments more quickly and without accessing the block chain. Now, however, people have become quite nervous about the idea and are worried that it puts too much trust in the bank.

Efficient micro-payments. A third example of Bitcoin scripts is a way to do efficient micro-payments. Say that Alice is a customer who wants to continually pay Bob small amounts of money for some service that Bob provides. For example, Bob may be Alice's wireless service provider, and requires her to pay a small fee for every minute that she talks on her phone.

Creating a Bitcoin transaction for every minute that Alice speaks on the phone won't work. That will create too many transactions, and the transaction fees add up. If the value of each one of these transactions is on the order of what the transaction fees are, Alice is going to be paying quite a high cost to do this.

What we'd like is to be able to combine all these small payments into one big payment at the end. It turns out that there's a neat way to do this. We start with a MULTISIG transaction that pays the maximum amount Alice would ever need to spend to an output requiring both Alice and Bob to sign to release the coins. Now, after the first minute that Alice has used the service, or the first time Alice needs to make a micropayment, she signs a transaction spending those coins that were sent to the MULTISIG address, sending one unit of payment to Bob and returning the rest to Alice. After the next minute of using the service, Alice signs another transaction, this time paying two units to Bob and sending the rest to herself. Notice these are signed only by Alice, and haven't been signed by Bob yet, nor are they being published to the block chain. Alice will keep sending these transactions to Bob every minute that she uses the service. Eventually, Alice will finish using the service, and tells Bob, "I'm done, please cut off my service." At this point Alice will stop signing additional transactions. Upon hearing this, Bob will say "Great. I'll disconnect your service, and I'll take that last transaction that you sent me, sign it, and publish that to the block chain."

Since each transaction was paying Bob a little bit more, and Alice a little bit less, the final transaction that Bob redeems pays him in full for the service that he provided and returns the rest of the money to Alice. All those transactions that Alice signed along the way won't make it to the block chain. Bob doesn't have to sign them. They'll just get discarded.

Technically all of these transactions are double-spends. So unlike the case with green addresses where we were specifically trying to avoid double-spends, with a strong guarantee, with this micro-payment protocol, we're actually generating a huge amount of potential double-spends. In practice, however, if both parties are operating normally, Bob will never sign any transaction but the last one, in which case the block chain won't actually see any attempt at a double-spend.

There's one other tricky detail: what if Bob never signs the last transaction? He may just say, "I'm happy to let the coins sit there in escrow forever," in which case, maybe the coins won't move, but Alice will lose the full value that she paid at the beginning. There's a very clever way to avoid this problem using a feature that we mentioned briefly earlier, and will explain now.

Lock time. T o avoid this problem, before the micro-payment protocol can even start, Alice and Bob will both sign a transaction which refunds all of Alice's money back to her, but the refund is "locked" until some time in the future. So after Alice signs, but before she broadcasts, the first MULTISIG transaction that puts her funds into escrow, she'll want to get this refund transaction from Bob and hold on to it. That guarantees that if she makes it to time t and Bob hasn't signed any of the small transactions that Alice has sent, Alice can publish this transaction which refunds all of the money directly to her.

What does it mean that it's locked until time t ? Recall when we looked at the metadata in Bitcoin transactions, that there was this lock_time parameter, which we had left unexplained. The way it works is that if you specify any value other than zero for the lock time, it tells miners not to publish the transaction until the specified lock time. The transaction will be invalid before either a specific block number, or a specific point in time, based on the timestamps that are put into blocks. So this is a way of preparing a transaction that can only be spent in the future if it isn't already spent by then. It works quite nicely in the micro-payment protocol as a safety valve for Alice to know that if Bob never signs, eventually she'll be able to get her money back.

Hopefully, these examples have shown you that we can do some neat stuff with Bitcoin scripts. We discussed three simple and practical examples, but there are many others that have been researched. One of them is multi-player lotteries, a very complicated multi-step protocol with lots of transactions having different lock times and escrows in case people cheat. There are also some neat protocols that utilize the scripting language to allow different people to get their coins together and mix them, so that it's harder to trace who owns which coin. We'll see that in detail in Chapter 6.

Smart contracts. T he general term for contracts like the ones we saw in this section is s mart contracts. These are contracts for which we have some degree of technical enforcement in Bitcoin, whereas traditionally they are enforced through laws or courts of arbitration. It's a really cool feature of Bitcoin that we can use scripts, miners, and transaction validation to realize the escrow protocol or the micro-payment protocol without needing a centralized authority.

Research into smart contracts goes far beyond the applications that we saw in this section. There are many types of smart contracts which people would like to be able to enforce but which aren't supported by the Bitcoin scripting language today. Or at least, nobody has come up with a creative way to implement them. As we saw, with a bit of creativity you can do quite a lot with the Bitcoin script as it currently stands.

12.4 Bitcoin blocks

So far in this chapter we've looked at how individual transactions are constructed and redeemed. But as we saw in chapter 2, transactions are grouped together into blocks. Why is this? Basically, it's an optimization. If miners had to come to consensus on each transaction individually, the rate at which new transactions could be accepted by the system would be much lower. Also, a hash chain of blocks is much shorter than a hash chain of transactions would be, since a large number of transactions can be put into each block. This will make it much more efficient to verify the block chain data structure.

The block chain is a clever combination of two different hash-based data structures. The first is a hash chain of blocks. Each block has a block header, a hash pointer to some transaction data, and a hash pointer to the previous block in the sequence. The second data structure is a per-block tree of all of the transactions that are included in that block. This is a Merkle tree and allows us to have a digest of all the transactions in the block in an efficient way. As we saw in Chapter 1, to prove that a transaction is included in a specific block, we can provide a path through the tree whose length is logarithmic in the number of transactions in the block. To recap, a block consists of header data followed by a list of transactions arranged in a tree structure.

Figure 3.8. T he Bitcoin block chain contains two different hash structures. The first is a hash chain of blocks that links the different blocks to one another. The second is internal to each block and is a

Merkle Tree of transactions within the blocks.

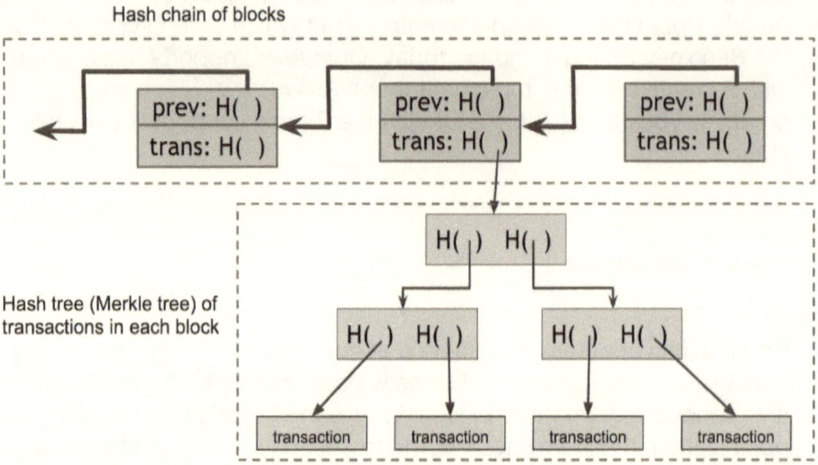

Hash chain of blocks

Hash tree (Merkle tree) of transactions in each block

The header mostly contains information related to the mining puzzle which we briefly discussed in the previous chapter and will revisit in Chapter 5. Recall that the hash of the block header has to start with a large number of zeros for the block to be valid. The header also contains a "nonce" that miners can change, a time stamp, and "bits", which is an indication of how difficult this block was to find. The header is the only thing that's hashed during mining. So to verify a chain of blocks, all we need to do is look at the headers. The only transaction data that's included in the header is the root of the transaction tree — the "mrkl_root" field.

"in":[{

},

"coinbase":"..." },

] "out":[

{"value":"25.03371419", "scriptPubKey":"OPDUPOPHASH160..."

}

]

***Figure 3.9.* c oinbase transaction.** A coinbase transaction creates
new coins. It does not redeem a previous output, and it has a null
hash pointer indicating this. It has a coinbase parameter which can
contain arbitrary data. The value of the coinbase transaction is the
block reward plus all of the transaction fees included in this block.

Another interesting thing about blocks is that they have a special
transaction in the Merkle tree called the "coinbase" transaction. This is
analogous to CreateCoins in Scroogecoin. So this is where the
creation of new coins in Bitcoin happens. It mostly looks like a normal
transaction but with several differences: (1) it always has a single input
and a single output, (2) the input doesn't redeem a previous output
and thus contains a null hash pointer, since it is minting new bitcoins
and not spending existing coins, (3) the value of the output is currently
a little over 25 Bitcoins. The output value is the miner's revenue from
the block. It consists of two components: a flat mining reward, which
is set by the system and which halves every 210,000 blocks (about 4
years), and the transaction fees collected from every transaction
included in the block. (4) There is a special "coinbase" parameter,
which is completely arbitrary — miners can put whatever they want in
there.

Famously, in the very first block ever mined in Bitcoin, the coinbase
parameter referenced a story in the Times of London newspaper
involving the Chancellor bailing out banks. This has been interpreted

"prev_out":{ "hash":"000000.....0000000", "n":4294967295

as political commentary on the motivation for starting Bitcoin. It also
serves as a sort of proof that the first block was mined after the story
came out on January 3, 2009. One way in which the coinbase
parameter has since been used is to signal support by miners for
different new features.

To get a better feel for the block format and transaction format, the best way is to explore the blockchain yourself . There are many web sites that make this data accessible , such as blockchain.info . Y o u can look at the graph of transactions, see which transactions redeem which other transactions, look for transactions with complicated scripts, and look at the block structure and see how blocks refer to other blocks. Since the block chain is a public data structure, developers have built pretty wrappers to explore it graphically.

12.5 The Bitcoin network

So far we've been talking about the ability for participants to publish a transaction and get it into the block chain as if this happens by magic. In fact this happens through the Bitcoin network. It's a peer-to-peer network, and it inherits many ideas from peer-to-peer networks that have been proposed for all sorts of other purposes. In the Bitcoin network, all nodes are equal. There is no hierarchy, and there are no special nodes or master nodes. It runs over TCP and has a random topology, where each node peers with other random nodes. New nodes can join at any time. In fact, you can download a Bitcoin client today, spin up your computer as a node, and it will have equal rights and capabilities as every other node on the Bitcoin network.

The network changes over time and is quite dynamic due to nodes entering and leaving. There isn't an explicit way to leave the network. Instead, if a node hasn't been heard from in a while — three hours is the duration that's hardcoded into the common clients — other nodes start to forget it. In this way, the network gracefully handles nodes going offline.

Recall that nodes connect to random peers and there is no geographic topology of any sort. Now say you launch a new node and want to join the network. You start with a simple message to one node that you know about. This is usually called your *s eed node*, and there are a few different ways you can look up lists of seed nodes to try connecting to. You send a special message, saying, "Tell me the

addresses of all the other nodes in the network that you know about."
You can repeat the process with the new nodes you learn about as
many times as you want. Then you can choose which ones to peer
with, and you'll be a fully functioning member of the Bitcoin network.
There are several steps that involve randomness, and the ideal
outcome is that you're peered with a random set of nodes. To join the
network, all you need to know is how to contact one node that's
already on the network.

What is the network good for? To maintain the block chain, of course.
So to publish a transaction, we want to get the entire network to hear
about it. This happens through a simple *f looding* algorithm,
sometimes called a *g ossip protocol*. If Alice wants to pay Bob some
money, her client creates and her node sends this transaction to all
the nodes it's peered with. Each of those nodes executes a series of
checks to determine whether or not to accept and relay the
transaction. If the checks pass, the node

in turn sends it to all of its peer nodes. Nodes that hear about a
transaction put it in a pool of transactions which they've heard about
but that aren't on the block chain yet. If a node hears about a
transaction that's already in its pool, it doesn't further broadcast it.
This ensures that the flooding protocol terminates and transactions
don't loop around the network forever. Remember that every
transaction is identified uniquely by its hash, so it's easy to look up a
transaction in the pool.

When nodes hear about a new transaction, how do they decide
whether or not they should propagate it? There are four checks. The
first and most important check is transaction validation — the
transaction must be valid with the current block chain. Nodes run the
script for each previous output being redeemed and ensure that the
scripts return true. Second, they check that the outputs being
redeemed here haven't already been spent. Third, they won't relay an
already-seen transaction, as mentioned earlier. Fourth, by default,
nodes will only accept and relay "standard" scripts based on a small
whitelist of scripts.

All these checks are just sanity checks. Well-behaving nodes all implement these to try to keep the network healthy and running properly, but there's no rule that says that nodes have to follow these specific steps. Since it's a peer-to-peer network, and anybody can join, there's always the possibility that a node might forward double-spends, non-standard transactions, or outright invalid transactions. That's why every node must do the checking for itself.

Since there is latency in the network, it's possible that nodes will end up with a different view of the pending transaction pool. This becomes particularly interesting and important when there is an attempted double-spend. Let's say Alice attempts to pay the same bitcoin to both Bob and Charlie, and sends out two transactions at roughly the same time. Some nodes will hear about the Alice → Bob transaction first while others will hear about the Alice → Charlie transaction first. When a node hears either of these transactions, it will add it to its transaction pool, and if it hears about the other one later it will look like a double-spend. The node will drop the latter transaction and won't relay it or add it to its transaction pool. As a result, the nodes will temporarily disagree on which transactions should be put into the next block. This is called a race condition.

The good news is that this is perfectly okay. Whoever mines the next block will essentially break the tie and decide which of those two pending transactions should end up being put permanently into a block. Let's say the Alice → Charlie transaction makes it into the block. When nodes with the Alice → Bob transaction hear about this block, they'll drop the transaction from their memory pools because it is a double-spend. When nodes with the Alice → Charlie transaction hear about this block, they'll drop the transaction from their memory pools because it's already made it into the block chain. So there will be no more disagreement once this block propagates to the network.

Since the default behavior is for nodes to hang onto whatever they hear first, network position matters. If two conflicting transactions or blocks get announced at two different positions in the network, they'll both begin to flood throughout the network and which transaction a node sees first will depend on where it is in the network.

Of course this assumes that every node implements this logic where they keep whatever they hear first. But there's no central authority enforcing this, and nodes are free to implement any other logic they want for choosing which transactions to keep and whether or not to forward a transaction. We'll look more closely at miner incentives in Chapter 5.

Sidebar: Zero-confirmation transactions and replace-by-fee. In Chapter 2 we looked at zero-confirmation transactions, where the recipient accepts the transaction as soon as it is broadcast on the network. This isn't designed to be secure against double spends. But as we saw, the default behavior for miners in the case of conflicting transactions is to include the transaction they received first, and this makes double-spending against zero-confirmation transactions moderately hard. As a result, and due to their convenience, zero-confirmation transactions have become common.

Since 2013, there has been interest in changing the default policy to *r eplace-by-fee* (RBF) whereby nodes will replace a pending transaction in their pool if they hear a conflicting transaction which includes a higher fee. This is the rational behavior for miners, at least in a short-term sense, as it gives them a better fee. However, replace-by-fee would make double-spending against zero-confirmation attacks far easier in practice.

Replace-by-fee has therefore attracted controversy, both in terms of the technical question of whether it is possible to prevent or deter double-spending in an RBF world, and the philosophical question of whether Bitcoin should try to support zero-confirmation as best it can, or abandon it. We won't dive into the long-running controversy here, but Bitcoin has recently adopted "opt-in" RBF whereby transactions can mark themselves (using the sequence-number field) as eligible for replacement by higher-fee transactions.

So far we've been mostly discussing propagation of transactions. The logic for announcing new blocks, whenever miners find a new block, is almost exactly the same as propagating a new transaction and it is all subject to the same race conditions. If two valid blocks are mined at the same time, only one of these can be included in the long term consensus chain. Ultimately, which of these blocks will be included will depend on which blocks the other nodes build on top of, and the one that does not get into the consensus chain will be orphaned.

Validating a block is more complex than validating transactions. In addition to validating the header and making sure that the hash value is in the acceptable range, nodes must validate every transaction included in the block. Finally, a node will forward a block only if it builds on the longest branch, based on its perspective of what the block chain (which is really a tree of blocks) looks like. This avoids forks building up. But just like with transactions, nodes can implement different logic if they want — they may relay blocks that aren't valid or blocks that build off of an earlier point in the block chain. This would build a fork, but that's okay. The protocol is designed to withstand that.

92

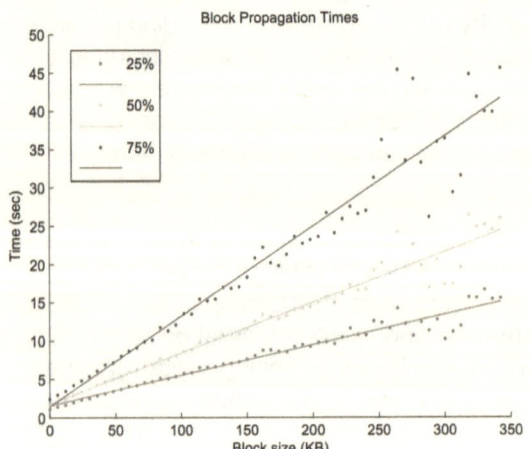

Source: Yonatan Sompolinsky and Aviv Zohar: "Accelerating Bitcoin's Transaction Processing" 2014

Figure 3.10 **B lock propagation time.** T his graph shows the average time that it takes a block to reach various percentages of the nodes in the network.

What is the latency of the flooding algorithm? The graph in Figure 3.10 shows the average time for new blocks to propagate to every node in the network. The three lines show the 25th, the 50th, and the 75th percentile block propagation time. As you can see, propagation time is basically proportional to the size of the block. This is because network bandwidth is the bottleneck. The larger blocks take over 30 seconds to propagate to most nodes in the network. So it isn't a particularly efficient protocol. On the Internet, 30 seconds is a pretty long time. In Bitcoin's design, having a simple network with little structure where nodes are equal and can come and go at any time took priority over efficiency. So a block may need to go through many nodes before it reaches the most distant nodes in the network. If the network were instead designed top-down for efficiency, we could make sure that the path between any two nodes is short.

Size of the network. I t is difficult to measure how big the network is since it is dynamic and there is no central authority. A number of researchers have come up with estimates. On the high end, some say that over a million IP addresses in a given month will, at some point, act, at least temporarily, as a Bitcoin node. On the other hand, there seem to be only about 5,000 to 10,000 nodes that are permanently connected and fully validate every transaction they hear. This may seem like a surprisingly low number, but as of this writing there is no evidence that the number of fully validating nodes is going up, and it may in fact be dropping.

Storage requirements. F ully validating nodes must stay permanently connected so as to hear about all the data. The longer a node is offline, the more catching up it will have to do when it rejoins the network. Such nodes also have to store the entire block chain and need a good network connection to be able to hear every new transaction and forward it to peers. The storage requirement is currently in the low tens of gigabytes (see Figure 3.11), well within the abilities of a single commodity desktop machine.

Figure 3.11. S ize of the block chain. F ully validating nodes must store the entire block chain, which as of the end of 2014 is over 26 gigabytes.

Finally, fully validating nodes must maintain the entire set of unspent transaction outputs, which are the coins available to be spent. Ideally this should be stored in RAM, so that upon hearing a new proposed transaction on the network, the node can quickly look up the transaction outputs that it's attempting to claim, run the scripts, see if the signatures are valid, and add the transaction to the transaction pool. As of mid-2014, there are over 44 million transactions on the block chain of which 12 million are unspent. Fortunately, that's still small enough to fit in less than a gigabyte of RAM in an efficient data structure.

Lightweight nodes. I n contrast to fully validating nodes, there are lightweight nodes, also called thin clients or Simple Payment Verification (SPV) clients. In fact, the vast majority of nodes on the Bitcoin network are lightweight nodes. These differ from fully validating nodes in that they don't store the entire block chain. They only store the pieces that they need to verify specific transactions that they care about. If you use a wallet program, it would typically incorporate an SPV node. The node downloads the block headers and transactions that represent payments to your addresses.

An SPV node doesn't have the security level of a fully validating node. Since the node has block headers, it can check that the blocks were difficult to mine, but it can't check to see that every transaction included in a block is actually valid because it doesn't have the transaction history and doesn't know the set of unspent transactions outputs. SPV nodes can only validate the transactions

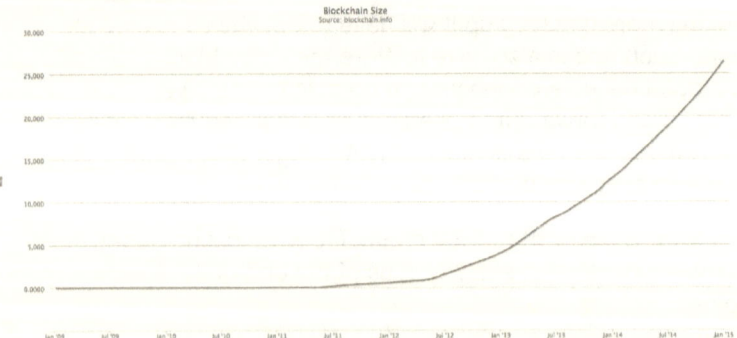

that actually affect them. So they're essentially trusting the fully validating nodes to have validated all the other transactions that are out there. This isn't a bad security trade off. They're assuming there are fully validating nodes out there that are doing the hard work, and that if miners went through the trouble to mine this block, which is a really expensive process, they probably also did some validation to make sure that this block wouldn't be rejected.

The cost savings of being an SPV node are huge. The block headers are only about 1/1,000 the size of the block chain. So instead of storing a few tens of gigabytes, it's only a few tens of megabytes. Even a smartphone can easily act as an SPV node in the Bitcoin network.

Since Bitcoin rests on an open protocol, ideally there would be many different implementations that interact with each other seamlessly. That way if there's a bad bug in one, it's not likely to bring down the entire network. The good news is that the protocol has been successfully re-implemented. There a r e i m p l e m e n t a t i o n s i n C + + a n d G o , a n d p e o p l e a r e w o r k i n g o n q u i t e a f e w o t h e r s . T h e b a d n e w s i s that most of the nodes on the network are running the bitcoind library, written in C++, maintained by the Bitcoin Core developers, and some of these nodes are running previous out-of-date versions that haven't been updated. In any event, most are running some variation of this one common client.

12.6 Limitations and improvements

Finally, we'll talk about some built-in limitations to the Bitcoin protocol, and why it's challenging to improve them. There are many constraints hard-coded into the Bitcoin protocol, which were chosen when Bitcoin was proposed in 2009, before anyone really had any idea that it might grow into a globally-important currency. Among them are the limits on the average time per block, the size of blocks, the number of signature operations in a block, and the divisibility of the currency, the total number of Bitcoins, and the block reward structure.

The limitations on the total number of Bitcoins in existence, as well as the structure of the mining rewards are very likely to never be changed because the economic implications of changing them are too great. Miners and investors have made big bets on the system assuming that the Bitcoin reward structure and the limited supply of Bitcoins will remain the way it was planned. If that changes, it will have large financial implications for people. So the community has basically agreed that those aspects, whether or not they were wisely chosen, will not change.

There are other changes that would seem to make everybody better off, because some initial design choices don't seem quite right with the benefit of hindsight. Chief among these are limits that affect the throughput of the system. How many transactions can the Bitcoin network process per second? This limitation comes from the hard coded limit on the size of blocks. Each block is limited to a megabyte, about a million bytes. Each transaction is at least 250 bytes. Dividing 1,000,000 by 250, we see that each block has a limit of 4,000 transactions, and given that blocks are found about every 10 minutes, we're left with about 7 transactions per second, which is all that the Bitcoin network can handle. It may seem that changing these limits would be a matter of tweaking a constant in a source code file somewhere. However, it's really hard to effect such a change in practice, for reasons that we will explain shortly.

So how does seven transactions per second compare? It's quite low compared to the throughput of any major credit card processor. Visa's network is said to handle about 2,000 transactions per second around the world on average, and capable of handling 10,000 transactions per second during busy periods. Even Paypal, which is newer and smaller than Visa, can handle 100 transactions per second at peak times. That's an order of magnitude more than Bitcoin.

Another limitation that people are worried about in the long term is that the choices of cryptographic algorithms in Bitcoin are fixed. There are only a couple of hash algorithms available, and only one signature algorithm, ECDSA, over a specific elliptic curve called secp256k1. There's some concern that over the lifetime of Bitcoin — which people hope will be very long — this algorithm might be broken.

BITCOIN OFFLINE VAULT WALLET – BA.NET

Cryptographers might come up with a clever new attack that we haven't foreseen which makes the algorithm insecure. The same is true of the hash functions; in fact, in the last decade hash functions have seen steady progress in cryptanalysis. SHA-1, which is included in Bitcoin, already has some known cryptographic weaknesses, albeit not fatal. To change this, we would have to extend the Bitcoin scripting language to support new cryptographic algorithms.

Changing the protocol. How can we go about introducing new features into the Bitcoin protocol? You might think that this is simple — just release a new version of the software, and tell all nodes to upgrade. In reality, though, this is quite complicated. In practice, it's impossible to assume that every node would upgrade. Some nodes in the network would fail to get the new software or fail to get it in time. The implications of having most nodes upgrade while some nodes are running the old version depends very much on the nature of the changes in the software. We can differentiate between two types of changes: those that would cause a *h ard fork* a nd those that would cause a *s oft fork*.

Hard forks. O ne type of change that we can make introduces new features that were previously considered invalid. That is, the new version of the software would recognize blocks as valid that the old software would reject. Now consider what happens when most nodes have upgraded, but some have not. Soon the longest branch will contain blocks that are considered invalid by the old nodes. So the old nodes will go off and work on a branch of the block chain that excludes blocks with the new feature. Until they upgrade their software, they'll consider their (shorter) branch to be the longest valid branch.

This type of change is called a hard forking change because it makes the block chain split. Every node in the network will be on one or the other side of it based on which version of the protocol it's running. Of course, the branches will never join together again. This is considered unacceptable by the community since old nodes would effectively be cut out of the Bitcoin network if they don't upgrade their software.

Soft forks. A second type of change that we can make to Bitcoin is adding features that make validation rules stricter. That is, they restrict the set of valid transactions or the set of valid blocks such that the old version would accept all of the blocks, whereas the new version would reject some. This type of change is called a soft fork, and it can avoid the permanent split that a hard fork introduces.

Consider what happens when we introduce a new version of the software with a soft forking change. The nodes running the new software will be enforcing some new, tighter, set of rules. Provided that the majority of nodes switch over to the new software, these nodes will be able to enforce the new rules. Introducing a soft fork relies on enough nodes switching to the new version of the protocol that they'll be able to enforce the new rules, knowing that the old nodes won't be able to enforce the new rules because they haven't heard of them yet.

There is a risk that old miners might mine invalid blocks because they include some transactions that are invalid under the new, stricter, rules. But the old nodes will at least figure out that some of their blocks are being rejected, even if they don't understand the reason. This might prompt their operators to upgrade their software. Furthermore, if their branch gets overtaken by the new miners, the old miners switch to it. That's because blocks considered valid by new miners are also considered valid by old miners. Thus, there won't be a hard fork; instead, there will be many small, temporary forks.

The classic example of a change that was made via soft fork is pay-to-script-hash, which we discussed earlier in this chapter. Pay-to-script-hash was not present in the first version of the Bitcoin protocol. This is a soft fork because from the view of the old nodes, a valid pay-to-script-hash transaction would still verify correctly. As interpreted by the old nodes, the script is simple — it hashes one data value and checks if the hash matches the value specified in the output script. Old nodes don't know to do the (now required) additional step of running that value itself to see if it is a valid script. We rely on new nodes to enforce the new rules, i.e. that the script actually redeems this transaction.

So what could we possibly add with a soft fork? Pay-to-script-hash was successful. It's also possible that new cryptographic schemes could be added by a soft fork. We could also add some extra metadata in the coinbase parameter that had some meaning. Today, any value is accepted in the coinbase parameter. But we could, in the future, say that the coinbase has to have some specific format. One idea that's been proposed is that, in each new block, the coinbase includes the Merkle root of a tree containing the entire set of unspent transactions. It would only result in a soft fork, because old nodes might mine a block that didn't have the required new coinbase parameter that got rejected by the network, but they would catch up and join the main chain that the network is mining.

Other changes might require a hard fork. Examples of this are adding new opcodes to Bitcoin, changing the limits on block or transactions size, or various bug fixes. Fixing the bug we discussed earlier, where the MULTISIG instruction pops an extra value off the stack, would also require a hard fork. That explains why, even though it's an annoying bug, it's much easier to leave it in the protocol and have people work around it rather than have a hard-fork change to Bitcoin. Hard forking changes, even though they would be nice, are very unlikely to happen within the current climate of Bitcoin. But many of these ideas have been tested out and proved to be successful in alternative cryptocurrencies, which start over from scratch.

13 BITCOIN SUMMARY OVERVIEW

Bitcoins are created as a reward for payment processing work in which users offer their computing power to verify and record payments into the public ledger. This activity is called mining and is rewarded by transaction fees and newly created bitcoins.

Bitcoin as a form of payment for products and services has grown, have warned that bitcoin users are not protected by refund rights or chargebacks.

The use of bitcoin by criminals has attracted the attention of financial regulators,

13.1.1   BLOCK CHAIN

The *block chain* is a public ledger that records bitcoin transactions. A novel solution accomplishes this without any trusted central authority: maintenance of the block chain is performed by a network of communicating nodes running bitcoin software.

13.1.2   UNITS

The unit of account of the bitcoin system is bitcoin. As of 2014 One *microbitcoin* equals to 0.000001 bitcoin, which is one millionth of bitcoin. A microbitcoin is sometimes referred to as a *bit*.

On 7 October 2014, the Bitcoin Foundation revealed a plan to apply for an ISO 4217 currency code for bitcoin,

13.1.3 OWNERSHIP

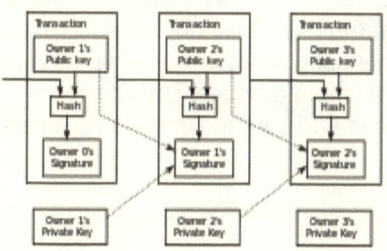

Simplified chain of ownership. In reality, a transaction can have more than one input and more than one output.

Ownership of bitcoins implies that a user can spend bitcoins associated with a specific address. To do so, a payer must digitally sign the transaction using the corresponding private key. Without knowledge of the private key the transaction cannot be signed and bitcoins cannot be spent. The network verifies the signature using the public key.

13.1.4 TRANSACTIONS

See also: Bitcoin network

A transaction must have one or more inputs. For the transaction to be valid, every input must be an unspent output of a previous transaction. Every input must be digitally signed. The use of multiple inputs corresponds to the use of multiple coins in a cash transaction. A transaction can also have multiple outputs, allowing one to make multiple payments in one go. A transaction output can be specified as an arbitrary multiple of satoshi. Similarly as in a cash transaction, the sum of inputs (coins used to pay) can exceed the intended sum of payments. In such case, an additional output is used, returning the change back to the payer. Any input satoshis not accounted for in the transaction outputs become the transaction fee.

To send money to a bitcoin address, users can click links on webpages; this is accomplished with a provisional bitcoin URI scheme using a template registered with IANA. Bitcoin clients like Electrum and Armory support bitcoin URIs. Mobile clients recognize bitcoin URIs in QR codes, so that the user does not have to type the bitcoin address and amount in manually. The QR code is generated from the user input based on the payment amount. The QR code is displayed on the mobile device screen and can be scanned by a second mobile device.

13.1.5 MINING

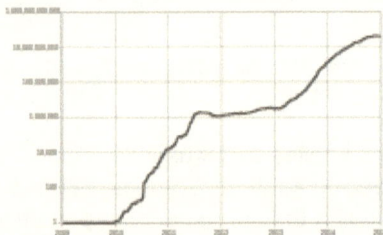

Relative mining difficulty from 2009-01-09 to 2014-12-31 (the difficulty scale is logarithmic). Relative mining difficulty is defined as the ratio between the difficulty target on 9 January 2009 and the current difficulty target.

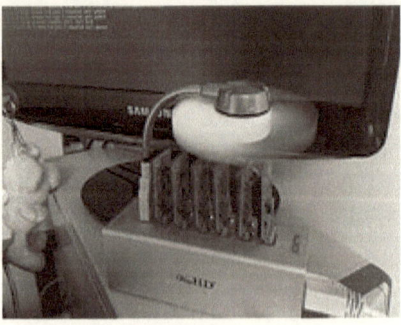

ASICMiner Block Erupter, a type of mining hardware used in 2013.

Mining is a record-keeping service.

In order to be accepted by the rest of the network, a new block must contain a so-called *proof-of-work*. The proof-of-work requires miners to find a number called a *nonce*, such that when the block content is hashed along with the nonce, the result is numerically smaller than the network's *difficulty target*.) before meeting the difficulty target.

Every 2016 blocks (approximately 14 days), the difficulty target is adjusted based on the network's recent performance, with the aim of keeping the average time between new blocks at ten minutes. In this way the system automatically adapts to the total amount of mining power on the network.

The proof-of-work system, alongside the chaining of blocks, makes modifications of the block chain extremely hard as an attacker must modify all subsequent blocks in order for the modifications of one block to be accepted. As new blocks are mined all the time, the difficulty of modifying a block increases as time passes and the number of subsequent blocks (also called *confirmations* of the given block) increases.

13.1.5.1   Practicalities

It has become common for miners to join organized mining pools,

The rewards of mining have led to ever-more-specialized technology being utilized. The most efficient mining hardware makes use of custom designed application-specific integrated circuits, which outperform general purpose CPUs while using less power.

As of 2015, even if all miners used energy efficient processes, the combined electricity consumption would be 1.46 terawatt-hours per year—equal to the consumption of about 135,000 American homes.

13.1.6   SUPPLY

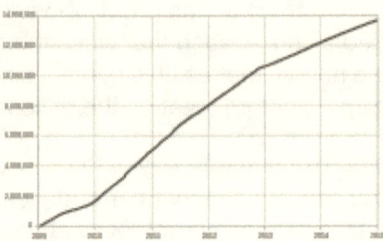

Total bitcoins in circulation. Horizontal axis: date ranging from 2009-01-09 to 2014-12-31.

The successful miner finding the new block is rewarded with newly created bitcoins and transaction fees.

13.1.7   TRANSACTION FEES

Paying a transaction fee is optional, but may speed up confirmation of the transaction.

13.1.8   WALLETS

See also: Digital wallet and Armory (software)

BA.net bitcoin wallet

Bitcoin paper wallet generated at ba.net

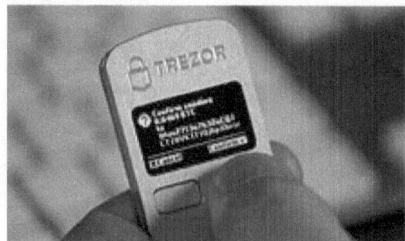

Trezor hardware wallet

A *wallet* stores the information necessary to transact bitcoins. While wallets are often described as a place to hold At its most basic, a wallet is a collection of these keys.

There are several types of wallet. *Software wallets* connect to the network and allow spending bitcoins in addition to holding the credentials that prove ownership.

13.1.8.1   *Reference implementation*

The first wallet program was released in 2009 by Satoshi Nakamoto as open-source code and was originally called bitcoind.

13.1.9   PRIVACY

Privacy is achieved by not identifying owners of bitcoin addresses while making other transaction data public. Bitcoin users are not identified by name, but transactions can be linked to individuals and companies.

13.1.10   FUNGIBILITY

Wallets and similar software technically handle bitcoins as equivalent, establishing the basic level of fungibility. Researchers have pointed out that the history of every single bitcoin is registered and publicly available in the block chain ledger, and that some users may refuse to accept bitcoins coming from controversial transactions, which would harm bitcoin's fungibility.

HISTORY

Main article: History of bitcoin

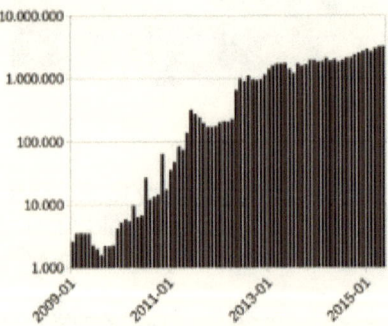

Number of bitcoin transactions per month (logarithmic scale)

Bitcoin was invented by Satoshi Nakamoto,

One of the first supporters, adopters, contributor to bitcoin and receiver of the first bitcoin transaction was programmer Hal Finney. Finney downloaded the bitcoin software the day it was released, and received 10 bitcoins from Nakamoto in the world's first bitcoin transaction.

Other early supporters were Wei Dai, creator of bitcoin predecessor *b-money*, and Nick Szabo, creator of bitcoin predecessor *bit gold*.

In 2010, an exploit in an early bitcoin client was found that allowed large numbers of bitcoins to be created.

Based on bitcoin's open source code, other cryptocurrencies started to emerge in 2011.

In March 2013, a technical glitch caused a fork in the block chain, with one half of the network adding blocks to one version of the chain and the other half adding to another. For six hours two bitcoin networks operated at the same time, each with its own version of the transaction history. The core developers called for a temporary halt to transactions, sparking a sharp sell-off.

In 2013 some mainstream websites began accepting bitcoins. WordPress had started in November 2012,)

In May 2013, the Department of Homeland Security seized assets belonging to the Mt. Gox exchange.

In October 2013, Chinese internet giant Baidu had allowed clients of website security services to pay with bitcoins.

The first bitcoin ATM was installed in October 2013 in Vancouver, British Columbia, Canada.

With about 12 million existing bitcoins in November 2013,

In the US two men were arrested in January 2014 on charges of money-laundering using bitcoins; one was Charlie Shrem, the head of now defunct bitcoin exchange BitInstant and a vice chairman of the Bitcoin Foundation. Shrem allegedly allowed the other arrested party to purchase large quantities of bitcoins for use on black-market websites.

In early February 2014, one of the largest bitcoin exchanges, Mt. Gox,

On June 18, 2014, it was announced that bitcoin payment service provider BitPay would become the new sponsor of St. Petersburg Bowl under a two-year deal, renamed the Bitcoin St. Petersburg Bowl.

Bitcoin was to be accepted for ticket and concession sales at the game as part of the sponsorship, and the sponsorship itself was also paid for using bitcoin.

Less than one year after the collapse of Mt. Gox, Bitstamp announced that the exchange would be taken offline while they investigate a hack which resulted in about 19,000 bitcoins (equivalent to roughly US$5 million at that time) being stolen from their hot wallet.

The bitcoin exchange service Coinbase launched the first regulated bitcoin exchange in 25 US states on January 26, 2015. At the time of the announcement, CEO Brian Armstrong stated that Coinbase intends to expand to thirty countries by the end of 2015.

ECONOMICS

13.1.11   CLASSIFICATION

According to the director of the Institute for Money, Technology and Financial Inclusion at the University of California-Irvine there is "an unsettled debate about whether bitcoin is a currency".

Economists define money as a store of value, a medium of exchange, and a unit of account and agree that bitcoin has some way to go to meet all these criteria.

Journalists and academics also dispute what to call bitcoin. Some media outlets do make a distinction between "real" money and bitcoins,

The People's Bank of China has stated that bitcoin "is fundamentally not a currency but an investment target".

13.1.12   BUYING AND SELLING

Bitcoins can be bought and sold both on- and offline. Participants in online exchanges offer bitcoin buy and sell bids. Using an online exchange to obtain bitcoins entails some risk, and, according to a study published in April 2013, 45% of exchanges fail and take client bitcoins with them.

13.1.13 PRICE AND VOLATILITY

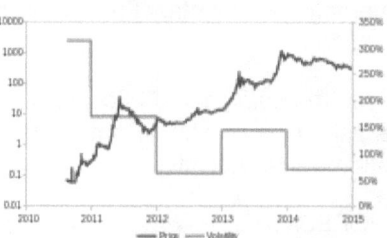

Price Left vertical axis: price, the scale is logarithmic. Right vertical axis: volatility. Horizontal axis: date ranging from 2010-08-17 to 2014-12-31.

To improve access to price information and increase transparency, on 30 April 2014 Bloomberg LP announced plans to list prices from bitcoin companies Kraken and Coinbase on its 320,000 subscription financial data terminals.

According to Mark T. Williams, as of 2014

Attempting to explain the high volatility, a group of Japanese scholars stated that there is no stabilization mechanism.

There are uses where volatility does not matter, such as online gambling, tipping, and international remittances.

The price of bitcoins has gone through various cycles of appreciation and depreciation referred to by some as bubbles and busts.

13.1.14 SPECULATIVE BUBBLE DISPUTE

Bitcoin has been labelled a *speculative bubble* by many including former Fed Chairman Alan Greenspan

13.1.15 PONZI SCHEME DISPUTE

Various journalists,

U.S. economist Nouriel Roubini, former senior adviser to the U.S. Treasury and the International Monetary Fund, has stated that bitcoin is "a Ponzi game".

Others have expressed the opinion that bitcoin is not a Ponzi scheme. The Huffington Post asked, "is bitcoin a Ponzi scheme, yes or no?" answering the question with a definitive "no!".

13.1.16   VALUE FORECASTS

Financial journalists and analysts, economists, and investors have attempted to predict the possible future value of bitcoin. In April 2013, economist John Quiggin stated, "bitcoins will attain their true value of zero sooner or later, but it is impossible to say when".

13.1.17   BITCOIN OBITUARIES

The "death" of bitcoin has been proclaimed numerous times.

13.1.18   RECEPTION

Some economists have responded positively to bitcoin, but many have not. François R. Velde, Senior Economist at the Chicago Fed described it as "an elegant solution to the problem of creating a digital currency".

David Andolfatto, Vice President at the Federal Reserve Bank of St. Louis, stated that bitcoin is a threat to the establishment, which he argues is a good thing for the Federal Reserve System and other central banks because it prompts these institutions to operate sound policies.

Free software movement activist Richard Stallman has criticized the lack of anonymity and called for reformed development.

Similarly, Peter Schiff, a bitcoin sceptic understands "the value of the technology as a payment platform" and his Euro Pacific Precious Metals fund partnered with BitPay in May 2014, because "a wire transfer of fiat funds can be slow and expensive for the customer".

Kevin Dowd, Professor of Finance and economics at Durham University has a bearish outlook on bitcoin. His presentation at the Cato Institute 2014 Annual Conference, Alternatives to Central Banking: Toward Free-Market Money, touched on bitcoin.

13.1.19   ACCEPTANCE BY MERCHANTS

Bitcoins are accepted in this café in the Netherlands as of 2013

In 2015, the number of merchants accepting bitcoin exceeded 100,000.

As of September 2014 PayPal allows North American merchants using its system the ability to receive payment in bitcoins.

Organizations accepting donations in bitcoin include: Greenpeace,

13.1.19.1 *Mainstream use of bitcoin*

As of February 2015

13.1.20   FINANCIAL INSTITUTIONS

Bitcoin companies have had difficulty opening traditional bank accounts because lenders have been leery of bitcoin's links to illicit activity.

One financial institution has been bullish on bitcoin. In a 2013 report, Bank of America Merrill Lynch stated that "we believe bitcoin can become a major means of payment for e-commerce and may emerge as a serious competitor to traditional money-transfer providers."

13.1.21 AS INVESTMENT

Some Argentinians have bought bitcoins to protect their savings against high inflation or the possibility that governments could confiscate savings accounts.

In 2013 and 2014, the European Banking Authority

In May 2015, Intercontinental Exchange Inc., parent company of the New York Stock Exchange, announced a bitcoin index initially based on data from Coinbase transactions.

13.1.22 VENTURE CAPITAL

Venture capitalists, such as Peter Thiel's Founders Fund, which invested US$3 million in BitPay, do not purchase bitcoins themselves, instead funding bitcoin infrastructure like companies that provide payment systems to merchants, exchanges, wallet services, etc.

13.1.23 POLITICAL ECONOMY

Bitcoin appeals to tech-savvy libertarians, because it so far exists outside the institutional banking system and the control of governments.

Bitcoin's appeal reaches from left wing critics, "who perceive the state and banking sector as representing the same elite interests, [...] recognising in it the potential for collective direct democratic governance of currency"

LEGAL STATUS AND REGULATION

In April 2013, Steven Strauss, a Harvard public policy professor, suggested that governments could outlaw bitcoin,

13.1.24   AUSTRALIA

Australia classifies bitcoin as property and an asset for capital gains purposes, however capital gains or losses arising from personal use of bitcoins is disregarded providing the cost of the bitcoins was less than $10,000.

13.1.25   CHINA

While private parties can hold and trade bitcoins in China, regulation prohibits financial firms like banks from doing the same.

13.1.26   EUROPEAN UNION

The European Central Bank classifies bitcoin as a convertible decentralized virtual currency.

13.1.27   ICELAND

As of 2014, foreign exchange activities with bitcoin are illegal in Iceland.

13.1.28   RUSSIA

CNBC reported that bitcoin was illegal in Russia in December, 2014,

13.1.29   TAIWAN

While bitcoin itself is not illegal here, bitcoin ATMs are prohibited.

13.1.30   THAILAND

In 2013, the Thai monetary authority, the Bank of Thailand, "issued a preliminary ruling that using bitcoins as described was illegal."

13.1.31   UNITED STATES

The U.S. Treasury classified bitcoin as a convertible decentralized virtual currency in 2013.

The U.S. Government Accountability Office (GAO) recommended in May 2013, that the Internal Revenue Service (IRS) formulate a tax guidance for bitcoin businesses.

In November 2013, the United States Senate held a committee hearing titled "Beyond Silk Road: Potential Risks, Threats and Promises of Virtual Currencies" to discuss virtual currencies.

The Federal Election Commission (FEC) deadlocked in November 2013 on whether to allow bitcoin in political campaigns with three Democrat members voting nay, three Republicans voting yea.

In May 2014, Brett Stapper, co-founder of Falcon Global Capital, registered to lobby members of Congress and federal agencies on issues related to bitcoin.

In January 2014, the U.S. Securities and Exchange Commission (SEC) focused on whether bitcoin-denominated stock exchanges were illegal, and inquired into unregistered securities offerings of the gambling site SatoshiDice and FeedZeBirds.

The U.S. Commodity Futures Trading Commission (CFTC) stated in March 2014 it considered regulation of digital currencies

In June 2014 California Assemblyman Roger Dickinson (D–Sacramento) submitted draft legislation (Assembly Bill 129) to legalize bitcoin and other forms of alternative and digital currency.

As of May 2015

13.1.32   VIETNAM

Vietnamese authorities have deemed bitcoin trading illegal.

CRIMINAL ACTIVITY

The use of bitcoin by criminals has attracted the attention of financial regulators, legislative bodies, law enforcement, and the media.

Several news outlets have asserted that the popularity of bitcoins hinges on the ability to use them to purchase illegal goods.

13.1.33   THEFT

There have been many cases of bitcoin theft.

Theft also occurs at sites bitcoins are used to purchase illicit goods. In late November 2013, an estimated $100 million in bitcoins were stolen from the online illicit goods marketplace Sheep Marketplace, which immediately closed.

Sites where users exchange bitcoins for cash are another target for theft. In late February 2014 Mt. Gox, one of the largest virtual currency exchanges, filed for bankruptcy in Tokyo amid reports that 744,000 bitcoins had been stolen.

13.1.34   BLACK MARKETS

A CMU researcher estimated that in 2012, 4.5% to 9% of all transactions on all exchanges in the world were for drug trades on a single deep web drugs market, Silk Road. are also available on black market sites that sell in bitcoin.

Several deep web black markets have been shut by authorities. In October 2013 Silk Road was shut down by U.S. law enforcement

Some black market sites may seek to steal bitcoins from customers. The bitcoin community branded one site, Sheep Marketplace, as a scam when it prevented withdrawals and shut down after an alleged bitcoins theft.

According to the Internet Watch Foundation, a U.K. based charity, bitcoin is used to purchase child pornography, and almost 200 such websites accept it as payment. Bitcoin isn't the sole way to purchase child pornography online, as Troels Oertling, head of the cybercrime unit at Europol, states, "Ukash and Paysafecard... have [also] been used to pay for such material." However, the Internet Watch Foundation lists around 30 sites that exclusively accept bitcoins.

13.1.35   MONEY LAUNDERING

Bitcoins may not be ideal for money laundering because all transactions are public.

13.1.36   PONZI SCHEME

In a Ponzi scheme that utilized bitcoins, The Bitcoin Savings and Trust promised investors up to 7 percent weekly interest, and raised at least 700,000 bitcoins from 2011 to 2012.

13.1.37   MALWARE

Bitcoin-related malware includes software that steals bitcoins from users using a variety of techniques, software that uses infected computers to mine bitcoins, and different types of ransomware, which disable computers or prevent files from being accessed until some payment is made. Security company Dell SecureWorks said in February 2014 that it had identified almost 150 types of bitcoin malware.

13.1.37.1 Unauthorized mining

In June 2011, Symantec warned about the possibility that botnets could mine covertly for bitcoins.

In mid-August 2011, bitcoin mining botnets were detected,

In April 2013, electronic sports organization E-Sports Entertainment was accused of hijacking 14,000 computers to mine bitcoins; the company later settled the case with the State of New Jersey.

German police arrested two people in December 2013 who customized existing botnet software to perform bitcoin mining, which police said had been used to mine at least $950,000 worth of bitcoins.

For four days in December 2013 and January 2014, Yahoo! Europe hosted an ad containing bitcoin mining malware that infected an estimated two million computers.

Several reports of employees or students using university or research computers to mine bitcoins have been published.

13.1.37.2 Malware stealing

Some malware can steal private keys for bitcoin wallets allowing the bitcoins themselves to be stolen. The most common type searches computers for cryptocurrency wallets to upload to a remote server where they can be cracked and their coins stolen. This method is effective because bitcoin transactions are irreversible.

One virus, spread through the Pony botnet, was reported in February 2014 to have stolen up to $220,000 in cryptocurrencies including bitcoins from 85 wallets.

A type of Mac malware active in August 2013, Bitvanity posed as a vanity wallet address generator and stole addresses and private keys from other bitcoin client software.

13.1.37.3 Ransomware

Another type of bitcoin-related malware is ransomware. One program called CryptoLocker, typically spread through legitimate-looking email attachments, encrypts the hard drive of an infected computer, then displays a countdown timer and demands a ransom, usually two bitcoins, to decrypt it.

SECURITY

Various potential attacks on the bitcoin network and its use as a payment system, real or theoretical, have been considered. The bitcoin protocol includes several features that protect it against some of those attacks, such as unauthorized spending, double spending, forging bitcoins, and tampering with the block chain. Other attacks, such as theft of private keys, require due care by users.

13.1.38   UNAUTHORIZED SPENDING

Unauthorized spending is mitigated by bitcoin's implementation of public-private key cryptography. When Alice sends a bitcoin to Bob, Bob becomes the new owner of the bitcoin. Eve observing the transaction might want to spend the bitcoin Bob just received, but she cannot sign the transaction without the knowledge of Bob's private key.

13.1.39   DOUBLE SPENDING

A specific problem that an internet payment system must solve is double-spending, whereby a user pays the same coin to two or more different recipients. An example of such a problem would be if Eve sent a bitcoin to Alice and later sent the same bitcoin to Bob. The bitcoin network guards against double-spending by recording all bitcoin transfers in a ledger (the block chain) that is visible to all users, and ensuring for all transferred bitcoins that they haven't been previously spent.

13.1.40   RACE ATTACK

If Eve offers to pay Alice a bitcoin in exchange for goods and signs a corresponding transaction, it is still possible that she also creates a different transaction at the same time sending the same bitcoin to Bob. By the rules, the network accepts only one of the transactions. This is called race attack, since there is a race which transaction will be accepted first. Alice can reduce the risk of race attack stipulating that she will not deliver the goods until Eve's payment to Alice appears in the block chain.

A variant race attack (which has been called a Finney attack by reference to Hal Finney) requires the participation of a miner. Instead of sending both payment requests (to pay Bob and Alice with the same coins) to the network, Eve issues only Alice's payment request to the network, while the accomplice tries to mine a block that includes the payment to Bob instead of Alice. There is a positive probability that the rogue miner will succeed before the network, in which case the payment to Alice will be rejected. As with the plain double-spending attack, Alice can reduce the risk of a Finney attack by waiting for the payment to be included in the block chain.

13.1.41   HISTORY MODIFICATION

The other principal way to steal bitcoins would be to modify block chain ledger entries.

For example, Eve could buy something from Alice, like a sofa, by adding a signed entry to the block chain ledger equivalent to *Eve pays Alice 100 bitcoins*. Later, after receiving the sofa, Eve could modify that block chain ledger entry to read instead: *Eve pays Alice 1 bitcoin*, or replace Alice's address by another of Eve's addresses. Digital signatures cannot prevent this attack: Eve can simply sign her entry again after modifying it.

To prevent modification attacks, each block of transactions that is added to the block chain includes a cryptographic hash code that is computed from the hash of the previous block as well as all the information in the block itself. When the bitcoin software notices two competing block chains, it will automatically assume that the chain with the greatest amount of work to produce it is the valid one. Therefore, in order to modify an already recorded transaction (as in the above example), the attacker would have to recalculate not just the modified block, but all the blocks after the modified one, until the modified chain contains more work than the legitimate chain that the rest of the network has been building in the meantime. Consequently, for this attack to succeed, the attacker must outperform the honest part of the network.

Each block that is added to the block chain, starting with the block containing a given transaction, is called a confirmation of that transaction. Ideally, merchants and services that receive payment in bitcoin should wait for at least one confirmation to be distributed over the network, before assuming that the payment was done. The more confirmations that the merchant waits for, the more difficult it is for an attacker to successfully reverse the transaction in a block chain — unless the attacker controls more than half the total network power, in which case it is called a 51% attack.

13.1.42   SELFISH MINING

This attack was first introduced by Ittay Eyal and Emin Gun Sirer at the beginning of November 2013. In this attack, the attacker finds blocks but does not broadcast them. Instead, the attacker mines their own private chain and eventually (when another miner or network of miners finds their own block) publishes several private blocks in a row. This forces the "honest" network to abandon their previous work and switch to the attacker's branch. As a result, honest miners lose a significant part of their revenue, while the attacker increases their profits due to changes in relative hashpowers.

According to the authors, a rational miner observing a selfish mining attacker would have an incentive to join the attacker's pool, thereby increasing the attacker's hashpower. This makes the attack and incentives even stronger, thus potentially leading to a 51% attack and the collapse of the currency.

Gavin Andresen and Ed Felten disagreed with this conclusion,

13.1.43   DEANONYMISATION OF CLIENTS

Along with transaction graph analysis, which may reveal connections between bitcoin addresses (pseudonyms),

NON-BITCOIN APPLICATIONS OF THE BLOCK CHAIN

In January 2015 IBM's Institute for Business Value announced ADEPT (Autonomous Decentralized Peer-to-Peer Telemetry) where network-connected devices can interact autonomously on the Internet of things using freely available technology including bittorrent, Telehash, and bitcoin.

In May 2015 NASDAQ announced its intention to use bitcoins of negligible value, called "colored coins", to represent and transfer pre-IPO trading shares on Nasdaq Private Markets.

BLOCK CHAIN SPAM

While it is possible to store any digital file in the block chain, the larger the transaction size the larger any associated fees become.

IN THE MEDIA

Several lighthearted songs celebrating bitcoin have been released.

In Season 3 CBS show *The Good Wife* featured an episode alluding to the creator of bitcoin as well as the FBI investigating the case. The episode titled 'Bitcoin for Dummies' was shown in early 2012.

A bitcoin documentary film called *The Rise and Rise of Bitcoin* was released in late 2014 and features interviews with people who use bitcoin such as a computer programmer and a drug dealer.

In the fall of 2014, undergraduate students at the Massachusetts Institute of Technology (MIT) each received bitcoins worth $100 "to better understand this emerging technology".

In early 2015, the CNN series *Inside Man* featured an episode about bitcoin. Filmed in July, 2014, it featured Morgan Spurlock living off of bitcoins for a week to figure out whether the world is ready for a new kind of money.

In science fiction novel *Neptune's Brood* by Charles Stross a modification of bitcoin is used as the universal interstellar payment system. The functioning of the system is a major plot element of the book.

14 HISTORY OF BITCOIN

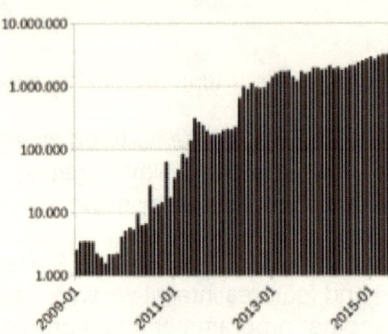

Number of Bitcoin transactions per month (logarithmic scale)

Bitcoin is a cryptocurrency, a form of money that uses cryptography to control its creation and management, rather than relying on central authorities. However, not all of the technologies and concepts that make up Bitcoin are new; the presumed pseudonymous Satoshi Nakamoto (the creator of Bitcoin, see below) integrated many existing ideas from the cypherpunk community when creating bitcoin.

CONTENTS

PRE-HISTORY

Prior to the release of Bitcoin there were a number of precursor ecash technologies starting with the issuer based ecash protocols of David Chaum and Stefan Brands, and moving on to distributed digital scarcity based ecash protocols starting from Adam Back's hashcash, Wei Dai's b-money, Nick Szabo's bit-gold and Hal Finney's RPOW which build on hashcash.

Independently and at around the same time Wei Dai proposed b-money Subsequently Hal Finney implemented and deployed RPOW a reusable form of hashcash based on IBM secure TPM hardware and remote attestation (centralized but with no issuer inflation risk).

Since the initial bit-gold proposal which proposed a collectible market based mechanism for inflation control Nick Szabo also investigated some additional enabling aspects for decentralized asset registers including Byzantine network issues.

There has been much speculation as to the identity of Satoshi Nakamoto with suspects including Wei Dai, Hal Finney and accompanying denials.

CREATION

In November 2008, a paper was posted on the internet under the name Satoshi Nakamoto titled *Bitcoin: A Peer-to-Peer Electronic Cash System*. This paper detailed methods of using a peer-to-peer network to generate what was described as "a system for electronic transactions without relying on trust".

On 6 August 2010, a major vulnerability in the bitcoin protocol was spotted. Transactions weren't properly verified before they were included in the transaction log or "block chain" which let users bypass bitcoin's economic restrictions and create an indefinite number of bitcoins.

GROWTH

Wikileaks

In January 2012, Bitcoin was featured as the main subject within a fictionalized trial on the CBS legal drama *The Good Wife* in the third season episode "Bitcoin for Dummies". The host of CNBC's *Mad Money*, Jim Cramer, played himself in a courtroom scene where he testifies that he doesn't consider bitcoin a true currency, saying "There's no central bank to regulate it; it's digital and functions completely peer to peer".

In October 2012, BitPay reported having over 1,000 merchants accepting bitcoin under its payment processing service.

In February 2013 the Bitcoin-based payment processor Coinbase reported selling US$1 million worth of bitcoins in a single month at over $22 per bitcoin.

In March the Bitcoin transaction log or "block chain" temporarily forked into two independent logs with differing rules on how transactions could be accepted. The Mt. Gox exchange briefly halted bitcoin deposits and the exchange rate briefly dipped by 23% to $37 as the event occurred

In April, payment processors *BitInstant* and *Mt. Gox* experienced processing delays due to insufficient capacity

Bitcoin gained greater recognition when services such as OkCupid and Foodler began accepting it for payment.

On 15 May 2013, the US authorities seized accounts associated with Mt. Gox after discovering that it had not registered as a money transmitter with FinCEN in the US.

On 23 June 2013, it was reported that the US Drug Enforcement Administration listed 11.02 bitcoins as a seized asset in a United States Department of Justice seizure notice pursuant to 21 U.S.C. § 881.

In July 2013 a project began in Kenya linking bitcoin with M-Pesa, a popular mobile payments system, in an experiment designed to spur innovative payments in Africa.

On 6 August 2013, Federal Judge Amos Mazzant of the Eastern District of Texas of the Fifth Circuit ruled that bitcoins are "a currency or a form of money" (specifically securities as defined by Federal Securities Laws), and as such were subject to the court's jurisdiction,

In October 2013, the FBI seized roughly 26,000 BTC from website Silk Road during the arrest of alleged owner Ross William Ulbricht.

Two companies, Robocoin and Bitcoiniacs launched the world's first bitcoin ATM on 29 October 2013 in Vancouver, BC, Canada, allowing clients to sell or purchase bitcoin currency at a downtown coffee shop.

In November 2013, the University of Nicosia announced that it would be accepting bitcoin as payment for tuition fees, with the university's chief financial officer calling it the "gold of tomorrow".

In September 2014 TeraExchange, LLC, received approval from the U.S.Commodity Futures Trading Commission "CFTC" to begin listing an over-the-counter swap product based on the price of a bitcoin. The CFTC swap product approval marks the first time a U.S. regulatory agency approved a bitcoin financial product.

PRICES AND VALUE HISTORY

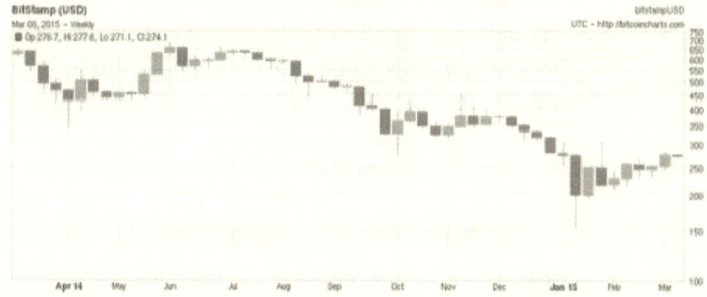

The price of a bitcoin reached an all-time high of US$1124.76 on 29 November 2013, up from just US$13.36 on 5 January at the start of the year; the price subsequently dropped into the $200-$300 range.

Among the factors which may have contributed to this rise were the European sovereign-debt crisis—particularly the 2012–2013 Cypriot financial crisis—statements by FinCEN improving the currency's legal standing and rising media and Internet interest.

As the market valuation of the total stock of bitcoins approached US$1 billion, some commentators called bitcoin prices a bubble. bitcoin passed a US$1000 all-time high on 28 November 2013 at MtGox.

Prices fell to around $400 in April 2014, before rallying in the middle of the year. They then declined to not much more than $200 in early 2015.

Until 2013 almost all market with bitcoins were in US $.

Bitcoin value history (comparison to US$)

Date	Price for 1 BTC	Notes
Jan 2009 – Jan 2010	basically none	No exchanges or market, users were mainly cryptography fans who were sending bitcoins for low or no value.
Feb 2010 – May 2010	less than $0.01	User "laszlo" made the first real-world transaction – he bought 2 pizzas for 10,000 BTC.
June 2010	$0.08	In five days, the price grew 1000%, rising from $0.008 to $0.08 for 1 bitcoin.
Feb 2011 – April 2011	$1	Bitcoin takes parity with US dollar.
8 July 2011	$31	top of first "bubble", followed by the first price drop
Dec 2011	$2	minimum after few months

Dec 2012	$13	slowly rising for a year
April 11, 2013	$266	top of a price rally, during which the value was growing by 5-10% daily.
May 2013	$130	basically stable, again slowly rising.
June 2013	$100	in June slowly dropping to $70, but rising in July to $110
Nov 2013	$350 – $1250	from October $150–$200 in November, rising to $400, then $600, eventually reaching $900 on 11/19/2013 and breaking $1000 threshold on 27 November 2013.
Dec 2013	$600 – $1000	Price crashed to $600, rebounded to $1,000, crashed again to the $500 range. Stabilized to the ~$650–$800 range.
Jan 2014	$750 – $1000	Price spiked to $1000 briefly, then settled in the $800–$900 range for the rest of the month.
Feb 2014	$550 – $750	Price fell following the shutdown of MTGOX before recovering to the $600–$700 range.
Mar 2014	$450 – $700	Price continued to fall due to a false report regarding bitcoin ban in China
Apr 2014	$340 – $530	The lowest price since the 2012–2013 Cypriot financial crisis had been reached at 3:25 AM on April 11
May 2014	$440 – $630	The downtrend first slow down and then reverse, increasing over 30% in the last days of May.
Mar 2015	$200 – $300	Price fell through to early 2015.

SATOSHI NAKAMOTO

Main article: Satoshi Nakamoto

"Satoshi Nakamoto" is presumed to be a pseudonym for the person or people who designed the original bitcoin protocol in 2008 and launched the network in 2009. Nakamoto was responsible for creating the majority of the official bitcoin software and was active in making modifications and posting technical information on the BitcoinTalk Forum.

Investigations into the real identity of Satoshi Nakamoto were attempted by *The New Yorker* and *Fast Company*. *The New Yorker's* investigation brought up at least two possible candidates: Michael Clear and Vili Lehdonvirta. *Fast Company*'s investigation brought up circumstantial evidence linking an encryption patent application filed by Neal King, Vladimir Oksman and Charles Bry on 15 August 2008, and the bitcoin.org domain name which was registered 72 hours later. The patent application (#20100042841) contained networking and encryption technologies similar to bitcoin's, and textual analysis revealed that the phrase "... computationally impractical to reverse" appeared in both the patent application and bitcoin's whitepaper.

Nakamoto's involvement with bitcoin does not appear to extend past mid-2010.

Stefan Thomas, a Swiss coder and active community member, graphed the time stamps for each of Nakamoto's 500-plus bitcoin forum posts; the resulting chart showed a steep decline to almost no posts between the hours of 5 a.m. and 11 a.m. Greenwich Mean Time. Because this pattern held true even on Saturdays and Sundays, it suggested that Nakamoto was asleep at this time, and the hours of 5 a.m. to 11 a.m. GMT are midnight to 6 a.m. Eastern Standard Time (North American Eastern Standard Time). Other clues suggested that Nakamoto was British: A newspaper headline he had encoded in the genesis block came from the UK-published newspaper *The Times*, and both his forum posts and his comments in the bitcoin source code used British English spellings, such as "optimise" and "colour".

An Internet search by an anonymous blogger of texts similar in writing to the bitcoin whitepaper suggests Nick Szabo's "bit gold" articles as having a similar author.

In a March 2014 article in *Newsweek*, journalist Leah McGrath Goodman doxed Dorian S. Nakamoto of Temple City, California, saying that Satoshi Nakamoto is the man's birth name.

THE FORK OF MARCH 2013

On 12 March 2013, a bitcoin miner running version 0.8.0 of the bitcoin software created a large invalid block. This created a split or "fork" in the block chain since computers with the recent version of the software accepted the invalid block and continued to build on the diverging chain, whereas older versions of the software rejected it and continued extending the block chain without the offending block. This split resulted in two separate transaction logs being formed without clear consensus, which allowed for the same funds to be spent differently on each chain. In response, the Mt. Gox exchange temporarily halted bitcoin deposits.

Miners resolved the split by downgrading to version 0.7, putting them back on track with the canonical blockchain. User funds largely remained unaffected and were available when network consensus was restored.

REGULATORY ISSUES

On 18 March 2013, the Financial Crimes Enforcement Network (or FinCEN), a bureau of the United States Department of the Treasury, issued a report regarding centralized and decentralized "virtual currencies" and their legal status within "money services business" (MSB) and Bank Secrecy Act regulations.

Additionally, FinCEN claimed regulation over American entities that manage bitcoins in a payment processor setting or as an exchanger: "In addition, a person is an exchanger and a money transmitter if the person accepts such de-centralized convertible virtual currency from one person and transmits it to another person as part of the acceptance and transfer of currency, funds, or other value that substitutes for currency."

In summary, FinCEN's decision would require bitcoin exchanges where bitcoins are traded for traditional currencies to disclose large transactions and suspicious activity, comply with money laundering regulations, and collect information about their customers as traditional financial institutions are required to do.

Patrick Murck of the Bitcoin Foundation criticized FinCEN's report as an "overreach" and claimed that FinCEN "cannot rely on this guidance in any enforcement action".

Jennifer Shasky Calvery, the director of FinCEN said, "Virtual currencies are subject to the same rules as other currencies. ... Basic money-services business rules apply here."

In its October 2012 study, *Virtual currency schemes*, the European Central Bank concluded that the growth of virtual currencies will continue, and, given the currencies' inherent price instability, lack of close regulation, and risk of illegal uses by anonymous users, the Bank warned that periodic examination of developments would be necessary to reassess risks.

In 2013, the U.S. Treasury extended its anti-money laundering regulations to processors of bitcoin transactions.

In June 2013, Bitcoin Foundation board member Jon Matonis wrote in *Forbes* that he received a warning letter from the California Department of Financial Institutions accusing the foundation of unlicensed money transmission. Matonis denied that the foundation is engaged in money transmission and said he viewed the case as "an opportunity to educate state regulators."

In late July 2013, the industry group Committee for the Establishment of the Digital Asset Transfer Authority began to form to set best practices and standards, to work with regulators and policymakers to adapt existing currency requirements to digital currency technology and business models and develop risk management standards.

In 2014, the U.S. Securities and Exchange Commission filed an administrative action against Erik T. Voorhees, for violating Securities Act Section 5 for publicly offering unregistered interests in two bitcoin websites in exchange for bitcoins.

THEFT AND EXCHANGE SHUTDOWNS

Theft of bitcoin has been documented on numerous occasions. At other times, bitcoin exchanges have shut down, taking their clients' bitcoins with them. A *Wired* study published April 2013 showed that 45 percent of bitcoin exchanges end up closing.

On 19 June 2011, a security breach of the Mt. Gox bitcoin exchange caused the nominal price of a bitcoin to fraudulently drop to one cent on the Mt. Gox exchange, after a hacker used credentials from a Mt. Gox auditor's compromised computer illegally to transfer a large number of bitcoins to himself. They used the exchange's software to sell them all nominally, creating a massive "ask" order at any price. Within minutes, the price reverted to its correct user-traded value.

In July 2011, the operator of Bitomat, the third-largest bitcoin exchange, announced that he lost access to his wallet.dat file with about 17,000 bitcoins (roughly equivalent to US$220,000 at that time). He announced that he would sell the service for the missing amount, aiming to use funds from the sale to refund his customers.

In August 2011, MyBitcoin, a now defunct bitcoin transaction processor, declared that it was hacked, which caused it to be shut down, paying 49% on customer deposits, leaving more than 78,000 bitcoins (equivalent to roughly US$800,000 at that time) unaccounted for.

In early August 2012, a lawsuit was filed in San Francisco court against Bitcoinica — a bitcoin trading venue — claiming about US$460,000 from the company. Bitcoinica was hacked twice in 2012, which led to allegations that the venue neglected the safety of customers' money and cheated them out of withdrawal requests.

In late August 2012, an operation titled Bitcoin Savings and Trust was shut down by the owner, leaving around US$5.6 million in bitcoin-based debts; this led to allegations that the operation was a Ponzi scheme.

In September 2012, Bitfloor, a bitcoin exchange, also reported being hacked, with 24,000 bitcoins (worth about US$250,000) stolen. As a result, Bitfloor suspended operations.

On 3 April 2013, Instawallet, a web-based wallet provider, was hacked,

On 11 August 2013, the Bitcoin Foundation announced that a bug in a pseudorandom number generator within the Android operating system had been exploited to steal from wallets generated by Android apps; fixes were provided 13 August 2013.

In October 2013, Inputs.io, an Australian-based bitcoin wallet provider was hacked with a loss of 4100 bitcoins, worth over A$1 million at time of theft. The service was run by the operator TradeFortress. Coinchat, the associated bitcoin chat room, has been taken over by a new admin.

On 26 October 23, a Hong-Kong based bitcoin trading platform owned by Global Bond Limited (GBL) vanished with 30 million yuan (US$5 million) from 500 investors.

On 3 March 2014, Flexcoin announced it was closing its doors because of a hack attack that took place the day before. Users can no longer log in to the site.

TAXATION AND REGULATION

In 2012, the Cryptocurrency Legal Advocacy Group (CLAG) stressed the importance for taxpayers to determine whether taxes are due on a bitcoin-related transaction based on whether one has experienced a "realization event": when a taxpayer has provided a service in exchange for bitcoins, a realization event has probably occurred and any gain or loss would likely be calculated using fair market values for the service provided."

In August 2013, the German Finance Ministry characterized bitcoin as a unit of account,

On 5 December 2013, the People's Bank of China announced in a press release regarding bitcoin regulation that whilst individuals in China are permitted to freely trade and exchange bitcoins as a commodity, it is prohibited for Chinese financial banks to operate using bitcoins or for bitcoins to be used as legal tender currency, and that entities dealing with bitcoins must track and report suspicious activity to prevent money laundering.

SPORTS SPONSORSHIP

On June 18, 2014, it was announced that Bitcoin payment service provider BitPay would become the new sponsor of St. Petersburg Bowl under a two-year deal, renamed the *Bitcoin St. Petersburg Bowl*. Bitcoin will be accepted for ticket and concession sales at the game as part of the sponsorship, and the sponsorship itself was also paid for using Bitcoin.

15 HD WALLETS HOW THEY WORK

With the rise of mobile wallets and the recent release of all these new hardware wallets, "HD wallets" have been getting a lot of attention lately. It seems like every hardware wallet has "HD," "BIP32" and/or

"BIP39" plastered all over their web site – but what does it really mean and why should you care? Is HD better somehow? What does "HD" even mean?

In the context of a Bitcoin wallet, "HD" usually stands for "Hierarchical Deterministic" – which probably doesn't help the non-programmers in the crowd all that much. Let's break down those terms:

- Hierarchical:
  Of the nature of a hierarchy; arranged in order of rank.

In the context of a Bitcoin wallet, this means that the addresses are in some way related to one another, specifically that you can use one bitcoin address to generate another, or that one can use a value called a "seed" to generate many related addresses.

- Deterministic:
  Describes a system in which no randomness is involved in the development of future states of the system.

This one is a straight-up programmer word that there's really no layman's equivalent to. Most programs begin with some input, do some stuff with it (usually math) and produce an output. A deterministic system is one in which the same input always results in the same output. Since this is the way that most math works the term is really only used when we're replacing something where random outputs are the norm.

Armed with a few good terms we can now discuss how HD wallets work, but if you want to understand why they're important you'll need to know one more thing: How the system they're replacing works.

We've discussed split-key cryptography and how it applies to Bitcoin before, in varying degrees of detail. We've even discussed the specific kind of cryptography Bitcoin uses in the kind of detail only a mathematician can love. What we haven't talked that much about are they keys themselves.

An encryption key is, basically, just a really big random number. It's such a big number chosen from such a large quantity of potential numbers that the likelihood of someone guessing your number is essentially zero. Bitcoin addresses are built from encryption keys and – importantly – the default way to make a new one is to simply choose it at random.

Choosing at random is the default for a lot of good reasons. We wouldn't want to choose a non-random number for the same reason that "Password123" is a very poor password: Patterns are easier to guess than randomness. Human brains aren't very good at producing random numbers and this makes human-chosen numbers really easy to guess. Letting a computer choose a number for you eliminates bias and ensures that your security isn't limited by your creativity. Unfortunately, it also comes with a downside: A bunch of unrelated random numbers are really hard to back up.

For a number of very good reasons, most Bitcoin implementations make use of "change addresses." This means that if you have 10 coins at address A and send 7 to address B, the "correct" thing to do with the change is send it to a new address, C. This has a number of positive implications for security and privacy, but it also makes backups difficult.

Imagine you backed up your wallet last week when all of your coins were at address A. Yesterday, you send those 7 coins to address B and your wallet software created a new change address C to hold the remaining 3 coins. Now your computer dies. Address C didn't exist at the time of your last backup, so those coins are lost. Forever.

The alternative is to make a ton of addresses at once and back them all up before they've been used. This is fine until you run out of addresses at which point you have to generate a bunch more and back them up all over again. For obvious reasons this is problematic – a difficult backup routine is one you're less likely to actually follow.

This is where HD wallets shine. Most implementations begin with a single "master key" commonly called a "seed." They use a "mnemonic" to represent the seed as a handful of simple words which you can write down or even memorize. Then, they use something like our old friend the hash function to generate a bunch of seemingly-random keys from the first one. By combining or otherwise modifying the master key with some incrementing value (seed+001, seed+002...) and pushing the result through a hash function you can get a bunch of addresses that look random, but are actually related to one another. We call these new Bitcoin addresses "child addresses." More importantly, since hashes are deterministic (there's that word again) you can always plug in the same master key and get the same seemingly-random keys back out.

In practice, it's a bit more complex than that – but even the simplified version should make the implications clear: An HD wallet can generate a basically-infinite number of Bitcoin addresses from a single seed and as long as you've got that seed backed up you can always use it to re-create the exact same Bitcoin addresses. Now, instead of having to pre-generate hundreds of keys or make near-constant backups, we can just write down a dozen or so words and chuck them in a fire safe. It's even feasible to memorize the words and keep a backup in your brain.

In practice, this makes the most difference in the mobile world. Because of the problems inherent to making secure backups of a phone wallet, most Android and iPhone Bitcoin wallets simply create and re-use a single address. There are a few security reasons to avoid this practice but it primarily represents a loss of privacy. Because you're always sending change back to your own address, most of the privacy benefits of Bitcoin are lost immediately.

This is important in the world of hardware wallets and cold storage. In both cases we're talking about a piece of hardware that will probably never have internet access or be allowed to communicate with another computer about what addresses it controls. Remember that each Bitcoin address you control is actually composed of two parts – a public key and a private key. In cold storage and hardware wallets, one device has all the private keys and the other has the corresponding public keys. Thanks to the ways private and public keys are related to one another we can do one more magical thing with an HD wallet: We can create a "master public key."

Just like we made that "one private key to rule them all" we can make its public counterpart – and it turns out that we can perform a similar "combine and hash" process on it to find all the child public keys that correspond to the child private keys from our earlier work. This means that with the master public key one device, like a computer, can figure out exactly which Bitcoin addresses you own – while an entirely separate device, like a Trezor or HW.1, can figure out the private keys that correspond to those addresses. All without having to communicate with one another.

As for "BIP32" and "BIP39" – they're just formal documents outlining the specific ways we go about making HD wallets. BIP32 covers the HD wallets themselves while BIP39 is a standard for mnemonics (converting keys to words and back again). These terms are there to let you know that the programmers didn't just make up their own methods that will disappear the moment their software goes defunct. For a backup to be good it has to still be usable a decade from now. Standards make that possible.

16   WHAT IS BITCOIN MULTISIG?

Multisig is a technique that allows several public keys to sign for the release of bitcoins. For example, Alice, Bob and Charlie can secure 1 BTC so that the agreement of only two of them is needed to spend it.

When Bitcoin was created, bitcoins could only be secured by using one public key. Using only one public key means that whoever knows the private key associated with that public key can spend the bitcoins it secures.

The no-single-point-of-failure rule, essential to reliable and secure systems, is not respected: the loss or revelation of a private key means the loss of bitcoins for the rightful owner.

A first practical solution for this problem was to use a known cryptographic method called secret sharing. It consists of breaking down a private key into independent parts (called shares). A fixed number of shares (less than the number of existing ones) can be used to reconstruct the private key. That way, the loss or revelation of a single share does not compromise the bitcoins. Also known as split wallets.

However, this does not plug well with the existing Bitcoin software: you have to use external tools to create and combine shares. Furthermore, in order to spend bitcoins, you have to gather a critical number of shares in one place, meaning that the no-single-point-of-failure rule isn't yet respected.

The solution was in the Bitcoin Core code all along. Included since the beginning but made non-standard, were two script operators allowing the use of multisignature with normal Bitcoin public keys. As the private keys needed to validate a multisignature transactions do not have to be gathered in the same place, security is greatly improved compared to using a single private key or cryptographic shares.

A Bitcoin Improvement Proposal, BIP 11, made this type of transaction standard but limited the maximum number of keys to 3. In

December 20th, 2011, BIP 11 support was added to the Bitcoin Core code and in late January 2012, the first BIP 11 type transactions appeared on the blockchain.

16.1.1.1   Multisig and Pay-to-script-hash

Even if multisig had been possible since early 2012 thanks to BIP 11, it really saw adoption thanks to another transaction type: pay-to-script-hash or P2SH. This new type made it possible to use arbitrary scripts to validate transactions. Before its introduction, only a restricted set of script types could be used to validate them.

With the possibility to execute arbitrary scripts, the maximum number of keys in a multisig script also increased from the maximum of 3 that BIP-11 type multisig accepted to the 15 compressed keys and corresponding signatures it's possible to pack in a P2SH script.

Most importantly, P2SH added a new Bitcoin address format. With BIP 11, you couldn't give an address for someone to send bitcoins to: you had to explicitly tell how to send bitcoins to your multisig setup (what keys, how many are needed to validate spending, how to order them, ...).

P2SH put using multisig on the same level of ease as using a single public key. This new technology, a great number of online wallets and software emerged, making using Bitcoin more secure.

16.1.1.2   Multisig today

More than 65.79 millions of bitcoins have been transacted using multisig, the great majority (more than 99%) using P2SH. This shows how vital P2SH has been to multisig adoption.

And now that more than 10% of bitcoins are secured by P2SH addresses (and most of them use multisig), it is safe to say that multisig took an very important place in the Bitcoin ecosystem in the last two years.

Among multisig's possible use cases, two emerges as the most popular:

- 2-of-3 multisig with 46.9 millions of BTC transacted by 1.1M addresses.
- 2-of-2 multisig with 13.3 millions of BTC transacted by 261,000 addresses.

It is however interesting to notice that among the 10 busiest P2SH addresses (those receiving and sending the most bitcoins), the top 4 uses 2-of-2 multisig, accounting for around 80% of all bitcoins transacted for 2-of-2 multisig. That makes 2-of-3 multisig the most commonly used multisig setup.

2-of-3 multisig is generally used by having a user generate two keys: one is saved as a backup, the other saved on a wallet ; the remaining key is created and stored by the wallet provider. To spend bitcoins, both the user and the wallet provider sign transactions. If the user or the wallet provider were to lose their key, the backup one can be used to move the funds, but it is impossible for the wallet provider to spend the user's funds.

16.1.1.3   Multisig Future

The release of Bitcoin Core 0.11.2 introduces a new script operator to the instruction set: OP_CHECKLOCKTIMEVERIFY, abbreviated to CLTV.

This new operator allows a transaction output to be made unspendable until some point in the future. While a similar feature is available through simply setting a transaction's locktime in the future, CLTV can be combined with other script instructions, like multisig or arithmetic operators, to create complex contracts.

For example, you could create a 2-of-3 multisig output that becomes a 1-of-3 after a given date. The introduction of CLTV is another step towards more complex Bitcoin uses.

Another important step that's taking shape right now is payment channels. A payment channel allows a party to make repeated micropayments to another party using multisig, without spamming the blockchain, only by publishing the first and the last transaction of the stream. Several variants of this idea, like the Lightning network, extend it to allow users to securely transact bitcoins through a network of payment channels without publishing every transaction to the blockchain.

17 BITCOIN:
A PEER-TO-PEER ELECTRONIC CASH SYSTEM
SATOSHI NAKAMOTO

17.1.1.1 October 31, 2008

ABSTRACT

A purely peer-to-peer version of electronic cash would allow online payments to be sent directly from one party to another without going through a financial institution. Digital signatures provide part of the solution, but the main benefits are lost if a trusted third party is still required to prevent double-spending. We propose a solution to the double-spending problem using a peer-to-peer network. The network timestamps transactions by hashing them into an ongoing chain of hash-based proof-of-work, forming a record that cannot be changed without redoing the proof-of-work. The longest chain not only serves as proof of the sequence of events witnessed, but proof that it came from the largest pool of CPU power. As long as a majority of CPU power is controlled by nodes that are not cooperating to attack the network, they'll generate the longest chain and outpace attackers. The network itself requires minimal structure. Messages are broadcast on a best effort basis, and nodes can leave and rejoin the network at will, accepting the longest proof-of-work chain as proof of what happened while they were gone.

1. INTRODUCTION

Commerce on the Internet has come to rely almost exclusively on financial institutions serving as trusted third parties to process electronic payments. While the system works well enough for most transactions, it still suffers from the inherent weaknesses of the trust based model. Completely non-reversible transactions are not really possible, since financial institutions cannot avoid mediating disputes. The cost of mediation increases transaction costs, limiting the minimum practical transaction size and cutting off the possibility for small casual transactions, and there is a broader cost in the loss of ability to make non-reversible payments for non-reversible services. With the possibility of reversal, the need for trust spreads. Merchants must be wary of their customers, hassling them for more information than they would otherwise need. A certain percentage of fraud is accepted as unavoidable. These costs and payment uncertainties can be avoided in person by using physical currency, but no mechanism exists to make payments over a communications channel without a trusted party.

What is needed is an electronic payment system based on cryptographic proof instead of trust, allowing any two willing parties to transact directly with each other without the need for a trusted third party. Transactions that are computationally impractical to reverse would protect sellers from fraud, and routine escrow mechanisms could easily be implemented to protect buyers. In this paper, we propose a solution to the double-spending problem using a peer-to-peer distributed timestamp server to generate computational proof of the chronological order of transactions. The system is secure as long as honest nodes collectively control more CPU power than any cooperating group of attacker nodes.

2. TRANSACTIONS

We define an electronic coin as a chain of digital signatures. Each owner transfers the coin to the next by digitally signing a hash of the previous transaction and the public key of the next owner and adding these to the end of the coin. A payee can verify the signatures to verify the chain of ownership.

The problem of course is the payee can't verify that one of the owners did not double-spend the coin. A common solution is to introduce a trusted central authority, or mint, that checks every transaction for double spending. After each transaction, the coin must be returned to the mint to issue a new coin, and only coins issued directly from the mint are trusted not to be double-spent. The problem with this solution is that the fate of the entire money system depends on the company running the mint, with every transaction having to go through them, just like a bank.

We need a way for the payee to know that the previous owners did not sign any earlier transactions. For our purposes, the earliest transaction is the one that counts, so we don't care about later attempts to double-spend. The only way to confirm the absence of a transaction is to be aware of all transactions. In the mint based model, the mint was aware of all transactions and decided which arrived first. To accomplish this without a trusted party, transactions must be publicly announced[1], and we need a system for participants to agree on a single history of the order in which they were received. The payee needs proof that at the time of each transaction, the majority of nodes agreed it was the first received.

3. TIMESTAMP SERVER

The solution we propose begins with a timestamp server. A timestamp server works by taking a hash of a block of items to be timestamped and widely publishing the hash, such as in a newspaper or Usenet post[2-5]. The timestamp proves that the data must have existed at the time, obviously, in order to get into the hash. Each timestamp includes the previous timestamp in its hash, forming a chain, with each additional timestamp reinforcing the ones before it.

4. PROOF-OF-WORK

To implement a distributed timestamp server on a peer-to-peer basis, we will need to use a proof-of-work system similar to Adam Back's Hashcash[6], rather than newspaper or Usenet posts. The proof-of-work involves scanning for a value that when hashed, such as with SHA-256, the hash begins with a number of zero bits. The average work required is exponential in the number of zero bits required and can be verified by executing a single hash.

For our timestamp network, we implement the proof-of-work by incrementing a nonce in the block until a value is found that gives the block's hash the required zero bits. Once the CPU effort has been expended to make it satisfy the proof-of-work, the block cannot be changed without redoing the work. As later blocks are chained after it, the work to change the block would include redoing all the blocks after it.

The proof-of-work also solves the problem of determining representation in majority decision making. If the majority were based on one-IP-address-one-vote, it could be subverted by anyone able to allocate many IPs. Proof-of-work is essentially one-CPU-one-vote. The majority decision is represented by the longest chain, which has the greatest proof-of-work effort invested in it. If a majority of CPU power is controlled by honest nodes, the honest chain will grow the fastest and outpace any competing chains. To modify a past block, an attacker would have to redo the proof-of-work of the block and all blocks after it and then catch up with and surpass the work of the honest nodes. We will show later that the probability of a slower attacker catching up diminishes exponentially as subsequent blocks are added.

To compensate for increasing hardware speed and varying interest in running nodes over time, the proof-of-work difficulty is determined by a moving average targeting an average number of blocks per hour. If they're generated too fast, the difficulty increases.

5. NETWORK

The steps to run the network are as follows:

1. New transactions are broadcast to all nodes.
2. Each node collects new transactions into a block.
3. Each node works on finding a difficult proof-of-work for its block.
4. When a node finds a proof-of-work, it broadcasts the block to all nodes.
5. Nodes accept the block only if all transactions in it are valid and not already spent.

6. Nodes express their acceptance of the block by working on creating the next block in the chain, using the hash of the accepted block as the previous hash.

Nodes always consider the longest chain to be the correct one and will keep working on extending it. If two nodes broadcast different versions of the next block simultaneously, some nodes may receive one or the other first. In that case, they work on the first one they received, but save the other branch in case it becomes longer. The tie will be broken when the next proof-of-work is found and one branch becomes longer; the nodes that were working on the other branch will then switch to the longer one.

New transaction broadcasts do not necessarily need to reach all nodes. As long as they reach many nodes, they will get into a block before long. Block broadcasts are also tolerant of dropped messages. If a node does not receive a block, it will request it when it receives the next block and realizes it missed one.

6. INCENTIVE

By convention, the first transaction in a block is a special transaction that starts a new coin owned by the creator of the block. This adds an incentive for nodes to support the network, and provides a way to initially distribute coins into circulation, since there is no central authority to issue them. The steady addition of a constant of amount of new coins is analogous to gold miners expending resources to add gold to circulation. In our case, it is CPU time and electricity that is expended.

The incentive can also be funded with transaction fees. If the output value of a transaction is less than its input value, the difference is a transaction fee that is added to the incentive value of the block containing the transaction. Once a predetermined number of coins have entered circulation, the incentive can transition entirely to transaction fees and be completely inflation free.

The incentive may help encourage nodes to stay honest. If a greedy attacker is able to assemble more CPU power than all the honest nodes, he would have to choose between using it to defraud people by stealing back his payments, or using it to generate new coins. He ought to find it more profitable to play by the rules, such rules that favour him with more new coins than everyone else combined, than to undermine the system and the validity of his own wealth.

7. RECLAIMING DISK SPACE

Once the latest transaction in a coin is buried under enough blocks, the spent transactions before it can be discarded to save disk space. To facilitate this without breaking the block's hash, transactions are hashed in a Merkle Tree [7][2][5], with only the root included in the block's hash. Old blocks can then be compacted by stubbing off branches of the tree. The interior hashes do not need to be stored.

A block header with no transactions would be about 80 bytes. If we suppose blocks are generated every 10 minutes, 80 bytes * 6 * 24 * 365 = 4.2MB per year. With computer systems typically selling with 2GB of RAM as of 2008, and Moore's Law predicting current growth of 1.2GB per year, storage should not be a problem even if the block headers must be kept in memory.

8. SIMPLIFIED PAYMENT VERIFICATION

It is possible to verify payments without running a full network node. A user only needs to keep a copy of the block headers of the longest proof-of-work chain, which he can get by querying network nodes until he's convinced he has the longest chain, and obtain the Merkle branch linking the transaction to the block it's timestamped in. He can't check the transaction for himself, but by linking it to a place in the chain, he can see that a network node has accepted it, and blocks added after it further confirm the network has accepted it.

As such, the verification is reliable as long as honest nodes control the network, but is more vulnerable if the network is overpowered by an attacker. While network nodes can verify transactions for themselves, the simplified method can be fooled by an attacker's fabricated transactions for as long as the attacker can continue to overpower the network. One strategy to protect against this would be to accept alerts from network nodes when they detect an invalid block, prompting the user's software to download the full block and alerted transactions to confirm the inconsistency. Businesses that receive frequent payments will probably still want to run their own nodes for more independent security and quicker verification.

9. COMBINING AND SPLITTING VALUE

Although it would be possible to handle coins individually, it would be unwieldy to make a separate transaction for every cent in a transfer. To allow value to be split and combined, transactions contain multiple inputs and outputs. Normally there will be either a single input from a larger previous transaction or multiple inputs combining smaller amounts, and at most two outputs: one for the payment, and one returning the change, if any, back to the sender.

It should be noted that fan-out, where a transaction depends on several transactions, and those transactions depend on many more, is not a problem here. There is never the need to extract a complete standalone copy of a transaction's history.

10. PRIVACY

The traditional banking model achieves a level of privacy by limiting access to information to the parties involved and the trusted third party. The necessity to announce all transactions publicly precludes this method, but privacy can still be maintained by breaking the flow of information in another place: by keeping public keys anonymous. The public can see that someone is sending an amount to someone else, but without information linking the transaction to anyone. This is similar to the level of information released by stock exchanges, where the time and size of individual trades, the "tape", is made public, but without telling who the parties were.

As an additional firewall, a new key pair should be used for each transaction to keep them from being linked to a common owner. Some linking is still unavoidable with multi-input transactions, which necessarily reveal that their inputs were owned by the same owner. The risk is that if the owner of a key is revealed, linking could reveal other transactions that belonged to the same owner.

11. CALCULATIONS

We consider the scenario of an attacker trying to generate an alternate chain faster than the honest chain. Even if this is accomplished, it does not throw the system open to arbitrary changes, such as creating value out of thin air or taking money that never belonged to the attacker. Nodes are not going to accept an invalid transaction as payment, and honest nodes will never accept a block containing them. An attacker can only try to change one of his own transactions to take back money he recently spent.

The race between the honest chain and an attacker chain can be characterized as a Binomial Random Walk. The success event is the honest chain being extended by one block, increasing its lead by +1, and the failure event is the attacker's chain being extended by one block, reducing the gap by -1.

The probability of an attacker catching up from a given deficit is analogous to a Gambler's Ruin problem. Suppose a gambler with unlimited credit starts at a deficit and plays potentially an infinite number of trials to try to reach breakeven. We can calculate the probability he ever reaches breakeven, or that an attacker ever catches up with the honest chain, as follows[8]:

$pqqz===$ probability an honest node finds the next block probability the attacker finds the next block probability the attacker will ever catch up from z blocks behind
$qz=\{1(q/p)zifp\leq qifp>q\}$

Given our assumption that $p>q$, the probability drops exponentially as the number of blocks the attacker has to catch up with increases. With the odds against him, if he doesn't make a lucky lunge forward early on, his chances become vanishingly small as he falls further behind.

We now consider how long the recipient of a new transaction needs to wait before being sufficiently certain the sender can't change the transaction. We assume the sender is an attacker who wants to make the recipient believe he paid him for a while, then switch it to pay back to himself after some time has passed. The receiver will be alerted when that happens, but the sender hopes it will be too late.

The receiver generates a new key pair and gives the public key to the sender shortly before signing. This prevents the sender from preparing a chain of blocks ahead of time by working on it continuously until he is lucky enough to get far enough ahead, then executing the transaction at that moment. Once the transaction is sent, the dishonest sender starts working in secret on a parallel chain containing an alternate version of his transaction.

The recipient waits until the transaction has been added to a block and z blocks have been linked after it. He doesn't know the exact amount of progress the attacker has made, but assuming the honest blocks took the average expected time per block, the attacker's potential progress will be a Poisson distribution with expected value:

$\lambda = zqp$

To get the probability the attacker could still catch up now, we multiply the Poisson density for each amount of progress he could have made by the probability he could catch up from that point:

$\sum_{k=0}^{\infty} \frac{\lambda^k e^{-\lambda}}{k!} \cdot \{(q/p)^{(z-k)} \text{ if } k \le z \text{ if } k > z\}$

Rearranging to avoid summing the infinite tail of the distribution...

$1 - \sum_{k=0}^{z} \frac{\lambda^k e^{-\lambda}}{k!}(1 - (q/p)^{(z-k)})$

Converting to C code...

```
#include  double AttackerSuccessProbability(double q, int z) {
       double p = 1.0 - q;    double lambda = z * (q / p);   double sum
= 1.0;  int i, k; for (k = 0; k <= z; k++)        {             double
poisson = exp(-lambda);          for (i = 1; i <= k; i++)                        poisson
```

Running some results, we can see the probability drop off exponentially with z.

q=0.1 z=0 P=1.0000000 z=1 P=0.2045873 z=2 P=0.0509779 z=3
P=0.0131722 z=4 P=0.0034552 z=5 P=0.0009137 z=6
P=0.0002428 z=7 P=0.0000647 z=8 P=0.0000173 z=9
P=0.0000046 z=10 P=0.0000012 q=0.3 z=0 P=1.0000000 z=5
P=0.1773523 z=10 P=0.0416605 z=15 P=0.0101008 z=20
P=0.0024804 z=25 P=0.0006132 z=30 P=0.0001522 z=35
P=0.0000379 z=40 P=0.0000095 z=45 P=0.0000024 z=50
P=0.0000006

Solving for P less than 0.1%...

P < 0.001 q=0.10 z=5 q=0.15 z=8 q=0.20 z=11 q=0.25 z=15
q=0.30 z=24 q=0.35 z=41 q=0.40 z=89 q=0.45 z=340

12. CONCLUSION

We have proposed a system for electronic transactions without relying
on trust. We started with the usual framework of coins made from
digital signatures, which provides strong control of ownership, but is
incomplete without a way to prevent double-spending. To solve this,
we proposed a peer-to-peer network using proof-of-work to record a
public history of transactions that quickly becomes computationally
impractical for an attacker to change if honest nodes control a
majority of CPU power. The network is robust in its unstructured
simplicity. Nodes work all at once with little coordination. They do not
need to be identified, since messages are not routed to any particular
place and only need to be delivered on a best effort basis. Nodes can
leave and rejoin the network at will, accepting the proof-of-work chain
as proof of what happened while they were gone. They vote with their
CPU power, expressing their acceptance of valid blocks by working
on extending them and rejecting invalid blocks by refusing to work on
them. Any needed rules and incentives can be enforced with this
consensus mechanism.

REFERENCES

1. W. Dai, "b-money," http://www.weidai.com/bmoney.txt, 1998. ↵
2. H. Massias, X.S. Avila, and J.-J. Quisquater, "Design of a secure
   timestamping service with minimal trust requirements," In 20TH
   SYMPOSIUM ON INFORMATION THEORY IN THE BENELUX,
   May 1999. ↵ ↵
3. S. Haber, W.S. Stornetta, "How to time-stamp a digital
   document," In JOURNAL OF CRYPTOLOGY, vol 3, no 2, pages
   99-111, 1991. ↵
4. D. Bayer, S. Haber, W.S. Stornetta, "Improving the efficiency
   and reliability of digital time-stamping," In SEQUENCES II:
   METHODS IN COMMUNICATION, SECURITY AND COMPUTER
   SCIENCE, pages 329-334, 1993. ↵
5. S. Haber, W.S. Stornetta, "Secure names for bit-strings," In
   PROCEEDINGS OF THE 4TH ACM CONFERENCE ON

COMPUTER AND COMMUNICATIONS SECURITY, pages 28-35, April 1997. ↵ ↵

6. A. Back, "Hashcash - a denial of service counter-measure," http://www.hashcash.org/papers/hashcash.pdf, 2002. ↵

7. R.C. Merkle, "Protocols for public key cryptosystems," In PROC. 1980 SYMPOSIUM ON SECURITY AND PRIVACY, IEEE Computer Society, pages 122-133, April 1980. ↵

8. W. Feller, "An introduction to probability theory and its applications," 1957. ↵

www.ingramcontent.com/pod-product-compliance
Lightning Source LLC
Chambersburg PA
CBHW031838170526
45157CB00001B/350